UNRAVELING

*The Patient-to-Patient's Guide Through
a Nervous Breakdown*

by Janine Baker

- **Depersonalization/Derealization**
- **Magical Thinking**
- **States of Consciousness**
- **Panic Attacks**
- **Anxious Rumination**
- **Obsessive Thoughts**
- **The Unconscious**
- **Identity Distortions**
- **Emotional Numbing**
- **Feelings of Unreality**

Copyright © 2004 by Janine Baker

All rights reserved. No part of this book shall be reproduced or transmitted in any form or by any means, electronic, mechanical, magnetic, photographic including photocopying, recording or by any information storage and retrieval system, without prior written permission of the publisher. No patent liability is assumed with respect to the use of the information contained herein. Although every precaution has been taken in the preparation of this book, the publisher and author assume no responsibility for errors or omissions. Neither is any liability assumed for damages resulting from the use of the information contained herein.

ISBN 0-7414-1978-5

Published by:

INFINITY
PUBLISHING.COM
1094 New Dehaven Street
Suite 100
West Conshohocken, PA 19428-2713
Info@buybooksontheweb.com
www.buybooksontheweb.com
Toll-free (877) BUY BOOK
Local Phone (610) 520-2500
Fax (610) 519-0261

Printed in the United States of America
Printed on Recycled Paper
Published May 2004

TABLE OF CONTENTS

Introduction to the Nervous Breakdown

If You're Terrified, Start Here 1
Blindsided: Out of Nowhere
Searching for Cause: Neurons or Neurosis? 10

Symptoms, Disorders, Syndromes
Descriptions of feelings 13
Ego-Syntonic or ego-Dystonic
Symptoms Chart

Disturbances of Emotion
Anxiety 21
Panic Attacks
Social Anxiety
Generalized Anxiety ("GAD")
Post-traumatic Stress
Depression 26
Mood swings

Disturbances of Thought
Cerebral Panic & Racing Thoughts 30
An Inner Monologue
Obsessions
Hypochondria
Rumination
Compulsions
Magical Thinking

Disturbances of Consciousness
Dissociative States 41
Depersonalization/Derealization
Questionnaire
Modes of Altered Consciousness

Picking Up The Pieces

The Kind of Person Who Comes Unraveled 58
    Chronic Fear of the Unknown
Hiding From the World/Hiding From Self

Recreational Drugs as Cause
Thoughts Too Strange to Tell
3 Things NOT to Do
    "I'll Do *Anything* to Feel Normal Again"
Long-term Sufferers
Suggestions

Seeking Help
2 Approaches to Treating Symptoms 83
Talking With a Doctor
Medication

Who's Who in Mental Health 93
    PROFESSIONALS CHART

Unraveling What Got Us Here 98
    THERAPY:
        Cognitive/Behavioral
        Psychodynamic
        Psychoanalytic-based

Towards Understanding The Mind
The Unconscious 108
    Symptom as Metaphor
Psychological Defenses – *"A Dangerous Patient"*
    The Mind's Coping Strategies

Learning Your Triggers 133
Suggestions II

Needing to Be Saner Than Sane
    As You Heal

I am not a doctor. In fact, I'm not a therapist of any kind. Not a professional in the mental health field. Never took a formal class on the subject.

But I'm a bit of an expert.

I've been there – right there – on what felt like the ledge of sanity. I was suffering a mental breakdown filled with some terrifying symptoms.

I'm a writer who was once very ill, and who worked damn hard to find a stable self. Along the way, I read, studied and questioned – constantly looking for answers, or at least some comprehension.

No one should be alone during a trip to hell. Although I had people who loved me and tried to help, none of us knew what we were doing.

I talked with doctors – but I felt they did not understand. Therapy did not work; most medications didn't touch it. Standing in large crowds of attempted support, I was totally alone.

In time, one psychiatrist reached me – and helped me clear a path to myself. Everyone's healing is unique, but the first step can be the discovery that someone else really hears what is happening to you.

I hope this book will be a companion in the darkest of nights for anyone trapped in the nightmare – especially those who were convinced that no one else could *ever* understand.

-- Janine

For my psychiatrist (a specialist in Reality) –
with gratitude & affection

Introduction

This is the night it will finally happen. For the past few months I've known it was coming... trying to prepare and praying that somehow it can be stopped. But I know. I know it. This is the night I am finally going insane.

*It's been a slow fading, -- like an old person's death -- but clearly worse, more sinister. Alive, alert, the body is sound. My **Self** is wafting off. Threads of me, every day, more threads like a ball of yarn...pull apart and drift across some room... the universe is unweaving me, and every morning I wake up and find less of me existing. I would scream in horror, but the part of me that could... is already gone. Buried alive. In the tomb of my own body.*

It's sadder than if I was dying, this vanishing. It's even what people say..."poor so-and-so...his mind is completely gone." Then so is the person.

In the bathroom mirror I stare at someone, someone like me, but it's not. The face in a mirror is... not... me. No human on earth could imagine this. I touch the face, and instantly it's not my own hand. Blind terror. Eyes that stare back, actually look calm. Of course no one can believe what's happening. They all tell me I just worry a lot - or that I think too much. People have always said that I think too much.

And when I talk to a doctor, I describe it as worry and nervousness. To avoid being around people, I say I'm under a lot of "stress." Those are words anyone can hear. But losing one's self -- watching reality slide away like rainwater -- that kind of thing scares people. Well, no kidding.

If You're Terrified, Start Here

Anxiety Symptoms
Will Not Kill You or
Make You Lose Your Mind

The human brain can produce terrifying states. During my worst fears, I was absolutely positive that I was going insane. That false belief was a fantasy at best, a delusion at worst. It was a morbid fear and unconscious wish – anything but a true perception. Yet at the time, nothing had ever felt more accurate.

Massive anxiety states are usually accompanied by fears of imminent: <u>Death and/or Insanity</u>

By all means, get a physical check-up - but once you receive a clean bill of health, take a good look at what anxiety can and cannot do.

It cannot kill you – plain and simple. You will believe it can, and you may claim to feel the life force literally slipping out of your body. You might have near-death sensations -- or such a profound sense of impending doom that you trust the premonition over any solid facts. You're still wrong.

Granted, when you have panic attacks with pounding heart, shortness of breath, trembling, chest tension, tingling in the hands and arms, lump in throat, constriction of neck, those physical sensations are real - not your imagination. They are biological responses occurring in your chest, in your throat, in your veins. However, being physically real does not mean they are signs of illness. You are experiencing the body's reaction to fear (conscious or otherwise), and producing healthy responses to perceived danger. No matter how intense those feelings become, they cannot kill you. The question is: *why are you so afraid?* (not *why is your body responding this way?*).

Anxiety will not summon a heart attack or burst a blood vessel. It will not cause enough oxygen deprivation to harm your brain. It cannot rupture organs or sever tissue.

Important: Those obsessive thoughts of impending doom are a **piece of your symptom**. Within the details of what you imagine is about to happen are some valuable clues to underlying fears.

The assault of a breakdown causes the mind to seek escape. And the stronger that wish becomes, the faster we develop a fear of dying/disappearing/losing self – which in turn, creates relentless self-observation. Caught in our own imaginations, unable to hide inside or outside, we become hyper-vigilant guards protecting a self that we know wants to vanish. It feels necessary – as if we are monitoring our own mental "death watch".

A fantasy of wanting to disappear or magically escape ordinary existence ("*I do not want to be in this body anymore*") can be a precursor to a consuming phobia. We try to counteract feelings of helplessness by *over*-inflating our power. If that works, we start to believe that we have amazing abilities, and soon start to worry that the strong *desire* to no longer exist could be enough to make it happen. Of course we know better – we are not insane…but at times we both know and *don't* know. That partial knowing is the trap making symptoms persist. Our own "harmless" magical thoughts have betrayed us.

Besides pounding heart and shortness of breath, anxiety states can produce bizarre *states of consciousness* –feelings of unreality or of being lost in a dream, frantic thoughts and a vanishing sense of self. Altered consciousness can feel very much like madness, but they are not psychosis (a break with reality, such as occurs in schizophrenia) and will not develop into psychosis.

An onslaught of emotions during already mounting anxiety can make you feel close to losing touch with reality. That is not what is happening, however. It feels *so* close – but it is an illusion.

You are no more susceptible to losing contact with reality than someone who has never had a single anxiety attack. Believing they're connected -- panic & psychosis -- is like fearing a bad ankle injury will develop into a heart attack. It could be argued that these both involve brain, not two different parts of the body, but it is still faulty logic. The mechanism causing crippling anxiety and the process that activates psychosis have nothing to do with each another – any more than an ankle is related to a heart. Terrible anxiety can only turn into worse anxiety -- as if that's not bad enough.

If you can realize that your symptoms are harmless, why not just ignore the sensations? If you *can*, by all means, do it. However, that never worked for me. Regardless of how many times my fears were de-mystified, explained, counteracted, I returned to my conviction that something was horribly wrong.

I might come home from a doctor's visit still clinging to reassurances…but by day's end, I was sensing new warning signs "*Oh, my God… this is it…it's finally happening…*"

Through my constant need for reassurance, I was begging for water to be poured into a leaking bucket. **No amount of words would ever be enough - because I was addicted to the process of being reassured.**

Doctor after doctor tried to explain it, but I could not accept that the ideas that terrified me were only symbols for a different unacknowledged fear. I fell asleep and woke up needing to hear "*no, you're not dying*" or "*no, won't lose your mind.*" That was all I thought about – and I 'knew' it was all that would ever matter. I was wrong.

Fears of death and insanity are decoys for threatening ideas lurking elsewhere in your mind.

Symptoms can function as impressive magic tricks that obscure our focus. The adage *trust your own instincts* is bad advice during a breakdown. *But I am inside my own mind – I can tell what's happening with me!* Don't be so sure.

Of course some readers will not believe me, and that's what makes us obsessive/anxiety patients so darn much fun – always believing ourselves the exception and refusing to be consoled for longer than a minute. (If you now think I must be addressing less serious cases than yours, consider that more proof -- you are *precisely* who this book is targeting).

Blindsided - The nightmare begins

In that second, nothing was real...I kept moving, walking too fast but couldn't slow down – nearly running through familiar stores – but unsure if I was running at all, only thinking of running...and everywhere, the faces were different...it seemed new people were working at every counter, but that wasn't possible. I recognized them and at the same time did not - alike, but no longer the same.

Buildings didn't looked right – like an old movie set of facades and cardboard. A sun glared way too bright in unworldly colors...and I was no longer awake, or not of this earth. I was positive I was suddenly dreaming – then the thought that I had died – didn't know I died and this was a holding pin... That was crazy, I knew that was crazy...

I tried not to scream... my mother standing next to me, seemed to turn into someone else. I had never used a drug in my life, but all I could think was that it was an acid trip - an alteration of consciousness so profound only a psychedelic could cause it. It was inconceivable that my own mind was doing this.

It can develop slowly or without any warning. The sudden ones come with a bonus fear – the belief that you can never again trust your own mind.

Mine began with a panic attack. On a sunny Friday morning, I walked down the front steps of my house. In the time it took to place a foot on the next step, my body was flooded with fear. From nowhere, thoughts scattered through my head faster than seemed humanly possible. I was under siege and the attacker was invisible. My mind was so threatened by *something* there seemed no choice but to die or go insane.

I told no one. Two days later - the same kind of attack, and it lasted longer. Hours later, my hands were shaking and my chest felt raw. By the third one, my thoughts had grown increasingly strange, and the idea arose that I actually could be losing my mind.

One afternoon I awoke from a nap to find that I could not *feel* awake. The room looked odd – everything seemed to exist in a dream. My own body felt unfamiliar – somehow "off center" – the room had an eerie quality to it, ominous and inexplicably foreign. There were no words to explain how something inside my perception had shifted. I walked around the house, trying to find something that could jar me awake – anything that might make me feel "present." But I seemed to be dream-walking in slow motion, as if under water.

Most nights I lay in bed, painfully sleepy but terrified of any transition – at all costs I dreaded the twilight state where I felt myself in between 2 worlds. The worst anxiety was anticipatory – unable to fall asleep for fear of waking up and feeling worse. I stayed home. I went out. Soon it no longer mattered what choices I made in the real world because something was happening inside me that defied it.

There are people with mental problems, and then there are the rest of us. We are the ones who can push through bad moods or worries. We are in control of our own minds.

Every day I seemed to be turning into someone else. When the fear was at its worst, I could not leave the house. Not that leaving the house was *difficult*, or that I had *trouble* doing it. I literally could not make myself walk through a door. Afraid of what could be "out there" – and at the same time, knowing better. Afraid that if I went too far from home, my mind could dissolve – and of course, I knew better. But at the mercy of my imagination, knowledge meant nothing. In less than two weeks, I had become mentally ill.

Nervous, yes…I'm just so nervous lately. That's all I knew to call it.

My façade was my only anchor – it seemed that by fooling everyone else I could somehow buy myself more time. I relied on excuses of *"feeling nauseous"* and *"family emergency"* to explain my sudden exits or failures to show up at all. No one can know. No one. *"I'm okay, I'm all right"* played over and over in my mind. *I'm still okay, still okay, it's okay..."* My purpose every day was to *will* myself into staying sane.

Within three months the anxiety became unbearable. When the masks wore out, I abandoned a college scholarship and spent a year inside the house. I lay in bed, crying and talking to my grandmother, pleading with God to just make it stop -- to give me a second chance, to let me have my life back. Some days were better than others, but nothing was right – and I assumed would never be right again.

The intensity of these bizarre states is astounding. A breakdown is more than an exaggeration of ordinary states of mind. One might expect anxiety or chronic sadness, daily crying, worrying, inability to concentrate. Although those are common symptoms, they are little preparation for the experience at hand.

The pervasiveness is unlike anything I had ever known. I was *watching* myself losing connection with the world. My senses were altered – things were too loud, too bright. I woke up every morning with a raging fear from my very core. When I looked at my arms, my hands, it was as if I had never seen them before that moment – and the obsession to keep looking, to keep checking for any sign of normalcy was relentless. The awareness that I was living inside a human body was so astonishing it shook my identity. I could remember other perspectives, but could not inhabit them. And without a doubt I knew - *of course this is insanity; of course it is.*

"...I have splintered -- like flakes of mercury scraped from the back of a mirror. I am here, and I am there, simultaneously - a patch, a torn shard...but nowhere in any of them do I exist." Holding someone's hand, I was consumed by the idea that the person could never be close *enough*. I needed the impossible – for someone to be inside my mind with me to witness the indescribable. I understood Sylvia Plath's metaphor of the "bell jar" – a glass dome fitting over our heads, forever separating human beings. There was never an identity. No connections. No relationships. I was alone in space. At night, the isolation was

physically painful - as if sharp ice was digging into my body. After a year I stopped believing I would ever get well.

NO ONE UNDERSTANDS

People will tell you *"there is nothing to be so afraid of."* They want you to realize that being out in public or having encounters with other people are not nearly as important as you fear. They will suggest that you might feel better if you could work, or go to school, and you should just *try* – do your best - no need to worry about what others think of you, no need to try to be perfect, etc. They think that is what you fear. They do not understand.

I remember running out of a job interview, in absolute terror – racing to the corner, frantically waving down a taxi to get me home, barely able to breathe or even to feel alive. I was not suffering from interview anxiety – I wasn't afraid of doing or saying the wrong thing or worried about what the interviewer thought. My fear was that I was seconds away from *dying* - literally dying on the spot – or that I was about to completely lose control of my mind. I felt myself dropping the reins to my own thoughts and actions, as if I might suddenly "become" someone else. I was vanishing, drifting into a netherland; it felt like my identity, my self was about to be overtaken by some other being – and within seconds, I would cease to exist.

Once we enter those symptom states, we are not afraid of anything real. We are obsessed with what seems to be happening inside our own minds. We fully realize that our thoughts are unreasonable yet we are being swept away and compelled to action by the feelings they produce. We are terrified of something inside ourselves - and no one else's words can touch it.

However, try to remember that the people who offer reassurances are well-meaning. They cannot understand how it feels because it is unlike any normal experience that humans encounter. Our isolation during those states adds to the horror, and encourages beliefs that we are beyond reach. Those are the symptoms of unraveling – nothing more and nothing less. They are horrible, but not precursors of anything permanent. You will not exist in this isolation forever. I remember the separation from everyone around me, and that no one, no matter how kind, ever came close to understanding. Your isolation is a temporary state. No one could doubt that more than I did. Yet, **it is temporary.**

But What Is *Happening* To Me?

There is much debate within psychiatry over exactly what occurs in the mind during a breakdown. A productive way to view it is this: you have developed some very disturbing feelings, thoughts and sensations. Those are the symptoms of your particular breakdown experience. Some people feel anxious, others get depressed, and some people experience both. Identifying your particular symptom-expressions will be important if you decide to try medication. Beyond that, the symptoms will not all fit together neatly to spell out a particular *problem*. The *problem* is that you broke down - and whatever treatment or recovery techniques you eventually choose will involve strengthening your core sense of self, the aspect of you that is most logical, mature and resilient – whether you suffer anxiety, depression, depersonalization, or obsessions/compulsions, etc.

Do not worry over what your unique set of symptom-experiences "means" – or why you are experiencing it this way and not another. That might sound counter-intuitive if you are comparing the apples and oranges of a *physical* medical problem with a mental one. In a physical disorder, specific details of a patient's condition serve as important clues for finding out "what's wrong" and "how to fix it." The internist needs to know precisely where the pain is, how long it lasts, and whether it feels acute, moderate, sharp, dull, throbbing, aching or burning. But emotional/mental symptoms fluctuate. Your condition may seem to get worse or improve greatly without any external provocation - it may appear that you are developing a whole *new* set of symptoms on top of your already-overwhelming repertoire. Your mind is just producing changes within the way it expresses its distress, as if finding new words to describe the already existing situation.

Naturally, it is important to be forthcoming with any mental health professional you talk with – describing your symptoms and their exact manifestation within your mind. However, most breakdown patients go way overboard in efforts to pinpoint the exact details of this mercurial experience. Remember the old-fashioned thermometers with the silver thread of mercury that seemed to vanish the closer you looked at it? Most symptoms can shimmer and hide in similar fashion. For anyone in breakdown mode, it is easy to get lost in self-observation and chronic self-monitoring.

SEARCHING FOR CAUSE

Nature/Nuture...
       Neurons or neurosis?

During the 1990's, the term *nervous breakdown* was replaced by "chemical imbalance." It represented a shift in widespread public belief that we suffer breakdowns as the direct result of irregularities within our brain's biochemistry. It is no longer our own doing -- not unconscious conflicts, or hidden thoughts or repressed wishes – it's pure chemicals.

Granted, a surplus or lack of the right neuro-transmissions can seriously affect our emotions. But the ways we consistently *think* also affect the neuro-chemical workings inside the brain. PET scans verify that people suffering mental symptoms have unusually high (or low) activity in specific regions of the brain. But that is not evidence that transmissions are malfunctioning. Psychiatry is left with the old chicken and egg conundrum. **In most cases, medical science simply does not know whether (1) the brain's organic chemical transmissions are malfunctioning and *causing* the trouble, or if (2) the brain's chemical changes are *normal responses to* troubled thinking within the mind/personality.**

The search for which is *cause* and which is *effect* has led to more questions, not conclusive answers. The truth you hear will depend on who you ask – without getting that disclaimer from either of them. Ardent theorists believe their own positions are empirically correct and quickly dismiss the alternate viewpoint. But after a century of debate, neither the bio-reductionist nor psychoanalyst can conclusively prove one case or disprove the other. Common sense suggests that truth hovers somewhere in the middle.

Why do some people endure terrible stress and never break down?
Why am I suddenly unable to control my thoughts and fears?

Where is all this coming from? What is happening inside my mind? and...

Why me?!

The answers probably lie in our genes.

Under massive stress, some minds grow depressed; some invoke anxiety; others dissociate. Most symptoms reflect our unique brain chemistries – a manifestation of latent possibilities carried since birth.

You did not inherit a destiny to come unraveled – but if it happens, your genetic "soft spots" probably determine which symptoms will develop.

Two gymnasts work out every day, pushing their endurance and testing the body's limits. If they consistently take shortcuts (improper alignment, favoring a stronger leg over the other) they are playing havoc with their bodies. Over time, the effect of wear and tear can push them to a breaking point.

One day the knees will give out, or a shoulder might dislocate. And it may happen during a routine workout on a day that was not stressful or unusual – just a final straw after years of risky habits.

But the two individuals will not have the same injuries – even if their workouts were identical. Everyone is born with genetic imprints of potential problems (akin to buying a computer with lots of software already installed. The software might get used one day, or might not. But its code resides on the hard drive and awaits activation).

Abuse the body, and unique genes will produce unique responses. A silent code for bad joints is activated in one athlete. Bone density weakness shows up in someone else. Repeated stress damages us in the precise way our genetic software predetermines.

Stress activates the latent gene map.

Nature *and* nurture.

Mental breakdowns are similar. Many of us were pushing emotional limits long before the breakdown occurred. We may have been living on the proverbial edge – with little leeway for human error, growth or change. We thought we had things under control. And in a way, we did – until the symptoms appear – and it all comes home to roost.

Symptoms, Disorders & Syndromes

"I read about any illness and it seems to describe me. Every mental symptom has started to sound familiar. I now relate to nothing in the ordinary world – but to every word within "Abnormal."

There is a veritable maze of medical terms to get lost in -- "syndromes," "primary/secondary symptoms," "ego syntonic/dystonic thoughts." I waded through all of it, convinced that once I found my own symptoms in a book, I would find the solution in pages that followed. In reality, that was just more fodder for obsession and worry. It is very useful to know the *basics* – to be able to recognize terminology and understand the gist of treatment concepts. Beyond that, some of us become so fascinated with theories of mind that we want to read the major psychiatric writers.

But be careful not to indulge in a frantic hunt to find yourself in a book. You may recognize some descriptions, but that is not the same thing as conclusive diagnosis. This is a very subjective science, and given the right frame of mind, *any* symptom can seem viable.

Symptoms commonly experienced during breakdowns include (but are not limited to) the following:

- Anxiety – depression – obsessions - mood swings – racing thoughts – constant worry – detachment from self - inability to concentrate or make decisions - emotional numbing - feelings of unreality – magical thinking – compulsions – panic -

We usually identify our symptoms as *complaints* -- thoughts or feelings that cause us great distress and inhibit our ability to function. We believe if we correctly describe them to a doctor, they will be recognized and fixed. But psychiatrists also listen for a distinction: *does this patient realize that all of his/her symptoms are symptoms? Or have some become incorporated into the person (who now believes in them as part of his/her own reality?), i.e., has a symptom become syntonic with the patient's ego?*

Ego-Syntonic – a thought or feeling that *seems to fit* with reality and my sense of self. It can cover the gamut from a high moral ideal to a colorful quirk - any trait or belief or feeling that I accept as part of myself -- anything I consider appropriate or justified, and not a sign of dysfunction.

Ego-alien – also called "ego-**dys**tonic". A feeling or thought that does *not* fit with my sense of reality or with the person I know myself to be. Most symptoms of a nervous breakdown will be ego-alien. Plagued by anxiety or feelings of unreality, we do not run to family members with the news that reality is shifting – because no matter how frightening, we fully realize the distortions are coming from within ourselves.

Ego-alien symptoms will send us to a doctor. Realizing something is wrong with our reactions/perceptions or feelings, we seek help – appreciating that the changes must occur inside ourselves.

On the other hand, an **ego-SYNtonic symptom** has become *integrated* within oneself. In its grip, the person believes the distorted reality. Ego-syntonic symptoms are common in more severe mental illness – in the case of psychotic hallucinations, paranoid delusions, etc. -- but they also exist in milder disorders. They are not indicators of severity, but of a patient's ability to reality test. It is an important distinction because poor reality testing can have serious implications if unnoticed.

> *Severely depressed people cannot see that their hopelessness is a symptom -- instead they believe despair and suicidal thoughts are justified responses to their current situation. A suicide attempt can result from the false belief that it is not illness, but the "horrible reality of life" that makes each day seem unbearable.*

Disorders

If you feel highly anxious, you definitely know it. But does that mean you have an anxiety *disorder*? Possibly, but not necessarily. If the anxiety is chronic, you might also feel depressed and begin obsessing about feeling so bad – does that indicate Depression and Obsessive/Compulsive Disorder on top of the original anxiety? Unlikely.

Granted, these symptoms can also be part of a diagnosis – just tack the word "disorder" at the end of its name. But someone can ruminate obsessively -- and may or may not have Obsessive Disorder. A person who feels very depressed may or may not have Major Depression.

An actual **diagnosis** requires a professional's eye and hinges on many factors, including how long the problem has persisted, presence or absence of additional symptoms, and the degree to which consistent functioning is impaired.

A **syndrome** is a cluster of symptoms that are forming a pattern, but not clearly pointing to a specific disorder. An *anxiety syndrome* means something different than a *depressive syndrome* - but neither give enough information to fit an established diagnosis.

Clear as mud? The field itself is hardly clear, and consumers need to realize that. In mental health sciences, descriptions blend into one another, and as a result, all diagnoses are somewhat subjective. Prioritizing symptoms and naming pathologies can also vary from doctor to doctor.

The most widely used criteria are found in The Diagnostic & Statistical Manual of Mental Disorders (usually called the "DSM") -- the reference bible of symptom categories.
The book is compiled by a panel of psychiatric authorities who revise/update it every four years.

The DSM is not purely objective either.

For an entry to be included, every word of the criteria must satisfy academic distinctions without contradicting any of the polar-opposite opinions of a diverse group of psychiatrists (the "DSM Committee"). Nothing done by committee is ever easy but with this many differing experts, it may be a miracle the book reaches print.

A few reasons not to self-diagnose:
- it won't help;
- it will make you more obsessive & self-monitoring;
- most people have an erratic combination of symptoms and some will stick around longer than others. Only time determines if any are chronic, and which vanish as fast as they appeared.

Bear in mind that official definitions originated from the mouths of *patients*. Sufferers reported their feelings to doctors, and after enough doctors heard similar accounts they coined a term – later modifying it when additional reports fit or failed to fit established categories.

In that regard, the patients wrote the book. And the book is far from finished. Medical experts only observe and assess what appears to constitute a specific disorder – based on words of people who are experiencing them. That is not some radical opinion of this author: it is precisely what most psychiatrists would tell you. We patients are the ones who invest psychiatry with much more power than it has. We are desperate to believe there are clear-cut scientific answers for our overwhelming feelings. We want to believe there is a name and treatment plan that will perfectly fit our unique set of symptoms. And we become outraged when it seems the doctor is refusing to tell us what we 'have', or fails to diagnose us ''right.' In reality, the experiences of a breakdown are so multi-layered and person-specific that the use of categories and terms are only helpful in the most general of ways (primarily for insurance companies). Plus, many of us are comforted to learn that other people have similar experiences, and some patients insist on a name/label for their collection of disturbing feelings. However, finding what it will take to recover (and how to manage symptoms until we do) takes time, trial-and-error and will be unique for each person. There is no microscope to pinpoint what is happening during a breakdown. And there is no universal formula for healing.

Psychiatry is a constantly changing science. Keep perspective.

Symptoms, Disorders and Syndromes

Symptoms Chart: The following is a quick reference of breakdown symptoms. The first column names the symptom or feeling state. The second column identifies diagnostic names for *disorders* that contain those symptoms (but this does not mean that everybody who has one from Column A must necessarily have the Column B disorder).

To refine things even more, symptoms fall into categories of origin. The third column identifies a symptom as "anxiety-*based*" or "a dissociative-*based* experience." These are not diagnoses, but shorthand terms for the suspected root of a symptom. This can be helpful in selecting medication(s).

Example: A patient complaining of feelings of unreality might have an underlying anxiety or an undiagnosed depression which could be the *primary symptom.* To treat the unreality feelings, the doctor looks for any broader symptom(s) that could be the source. Are the unreal feelings episodic? Possible responses to panic? (both of which point to *anxiety*-based experience, making anxiety the logical treatment target).

Or the sensations may be chronic with additional disturbances of deadened emotions, lethargy and detachment (all pointing to a *mood-based* condition such as depression). Of course solutions are rarely that obvious, and investigations are much more involved.

Here it gets tricky. A symptom can be labeled "anxiety-based" without the sufferer *feeling* anxious at all. This creates murky communication between doctor and patient – a doctor calls a symptom "depressive" while the patient denies feeling even remotely depressed. Remember the logic: the basis of any symptom can be a seemingly unrelated dormant condition – and the *noticeable* symptom is serving as camouflage.

In a physical disorder, symptoms are relatively straightforward. We have no doubts that a stomach pain indicates something wrong in the stomach – and never question if it might really be an eye injury that we are redirecting to the belly. However, *mental* symptoms play precisely those games with detectives trying to ferret them out.

If a doctor seems to discount your opinions, it may be due to that assessment of underlying symptoms. The doctor probably believes you, but may suspect you are being misled by the trickery of your own illness. (An excellent psychiatrist will explain this – but most professionals in any field are not excellent, but average. It helps to be armed with consumer knowledge).

Symptoms Chart

Symptom	Related Disorders	Possible basis:
Chronic anxiety	Generalized anxiety disorder (GAD)	- Anxiety based and/or Depression based
Panic attacks	- Panic disorder - Post traumatic stress disorder	- Anxiety based
Phobia(s)	- Phobic disorder	- Anxiety based - Depression based
Social phobia	- Social anxiety disorder - Depressive disorder	- Anxiety based - Depression based
*Cerebral Panic	* author's term, not official description	- Anxiety based - Dissociative reaction
Obsessive thoughts, ruminations	- Obsessive/compulsive - GAD - Depressive disorder	- Anxiety based - Depression based (maybe bio-chemically triggered)
Compulsions	- Obsessive/compulsive - GAD - Depressive disorder	- Anxiety based - Depression based (maybe bio-chemical)
Depersonalization	- Depersonalization disorder - Anxiety or panic disorder - Post-traumatic stress - Depressive Disorder	- Dissociative reaction &/or Anxiety based and/or Depressive response
Derealization	- Depressive Disorder - Post-traumatic stress disorder - Anxiety or panic disorder	- Dissociative reaction &/or Anxiety based and/or Depressive response

Anxiety States

Generally, anxiety implies a state of apprehensive fear – obsessive worry that something bad will happen, or *might* happen. But the definition is dependent on who does the defining.

A biological-reductionist may presume *anxiety* is the neuro-chemical response to "fight or flight" stimulus. (such as panic attacks);

A psychoanalytic therapist will view anxiety as part of the human condition. The *disturbance* comes from our inability to *handle* the uncertainties of reality, or from unconscious conflicts that are perceived as threatening. "An inability to tolerate anxiety" refers to the failure of our normal defenses to buffer us from disturbing thoughts. In a very loose metaphor, we suddenly find ourselves pressed against the glass of *too*-much-reality and are unable to look away. At that moment, we thicken the glass that serves as boundary between self and the disturbing truths, and the thicker the glass, the more intense our symptoms. The problem lies not in *feeling* anxious, but from the machinations performed in the name of avoiding it.

Panic Attack

It can strike in the most familiar surroundings – shopping in a neighborhood store, driving a regular route to work, standing in line at the bank. One instant you're contemplating weekend plans, and in the next you're thrust into a mounting state of terror. Heart pounding, faster and faster...you're feeling it move inside your chest...never felt anything like it ... can barely breathe...the environment looks odd, not real....hands feel numb, hot then cold...it's a heart attack [or rapidly approaching madness]....but it is without a doubt...complete and utter....loss of control over your own body and mind.

That's panic – a form of anxiety symptom that arrives like an assault, peaks, and then vanishes. Half an hour later, you'll feel normal again. Physically normal, that is. Mentally, you might have strong and lingering fears. "*What was that*?!" plays over and over inside the mind, and you grow obsessed with the factors that seemed to precede it. That is where the real damage gets done.

Avoidance behavior may follow – decisions to stay away from the place (or type of place) where you had the panic. While that feels logical, it will soon breed more symptoms. The anxiety that caused your panic has to do with what is in your *thoughts* -- not anything in that *store*. Or on that block. Or in that general area of town. Avoidance can quickly spread to include every location beyond the living room.

Social anxiety:
Usually defined as intense anxiety in social situations; fears of being judged, rejected, or criticized lead to avoidance of close contact with other people (to prevent more anxiety). Over time, isolation may stir up depressive feelings and increased worries at the thought of interacting with anyone outside the immediate family. The term "Social Anxiety" is often over- used to describe any fear falling into the social arena – phobias of public speaking, stage fright, panic under performance. But in those instances, the situation provoking the reaction is extreme. That is very different from being unable to maintain ordinary interactions with other people without feeling massive anxiety.

The basis of Social Anxiety may not be anxiety at all, but depression. When someone becomes increasingly withdrawn, the self-image grows increasingly vulnerable. The fewer encounters we have with other people, the more we have riding on those encounters. Scarce moments of connection become matters of life and death; a single slight (if the only risk taken all year) can be devastating. Eventually the prospect of rejection is so overwhelming that the person despairs of ever feeling sturdy enough to endure relationships. Withdrawal leads to isolation, and the prophecy fulfills itself.

Bear in mind that during a breakdown, most patients will try to avoid being with other people. Some develop a fear of strangers and/or worry obsessively about being judged or ridiculed by what they consider "normal" others. But that kind of social avoidance is a direct result of *other* symptoms, not a state of mind that was chronic before the breakdown occurred.

Agoraphobia

Intense anxiety at the thought of being in a public place, (and often without the company of a particular person whose presence provides stability). Usually includes at least one panic attack that occurred under similar circumstances prior to developing the phobia. These patients become literal prisoners of their fears, because what seemed like a temporary solution (till things get better) turns into a daily ground of being.

It is an *illusion* that the source of the fear is out there and not inside our own mind. This is a hallmark of phobias in general. *"As long as I can avoid "X" I am okay. My terror is confined to a specific activity or object. Avoid it, and I can avoid my fears."*

Haunted by memories of the sudden attack, you spend a great deal of energy trying to figure out how to avoid ever having another one. Unfortunately, it's highly possible you will have another, and again, it will seem to come from nowhere. If life has been unusually stressful prior to the panic attack, you may consider it proof that everything had become too much. Then common sense will tell you to make changes - slow down, delegate, change perspective, etc.

But if life has been relatively smooth, a breakdown may be even more disturbing. *"Why now?! Things in my life are gong well - how could this happen? I must have something physically wrong."*

Something Is Wrong With My Nervous System

It never hurts to see a doctor and rule out physical problems. But I promise that the majority of people with these types of anxiety symptoms are experiencing them in response to an emotional/psychological problem.

The word *neurosis* does not sit well with most of us. In fact, it grew so unpopular that the DSM finally replaced it with a kinder term - disorder. Most of us prefer a physical explanation for our pain, and *disorder* implies a problem that will garner respect. If we have something chemically wrong, a doctor can adjust -- or *re*-order us -- and we will be fine again. But to consider that somehow, without meaning to, we keep bringing these feelings out of ourselves? That can seem way too daunting to solve.

Certain emotional/mental conditions do have strong physical/chemical components. But I believe there is far too much current emphasis on the physical aspect of symptoms and not enough on our unconscious thought processes. Thoughts alone play powerful roles in the creation of symptoms.

In suggesting psychological causes, I do not mean that what you feel is *imaginary* - or "*all in your head*". And I realize that you are not choosing to feel this way. But the mind is capable of producing remarkable states as attempted solutions to conflicts within our thinking. In that sense, a breakdown can be more of a breaking *out* for a self that can no longer maintain its fragile status quo -- one originally built on magical thinking, facades and inhibitions.

When everything feels frighteningly unreal, it may actually be reality trying to break through.

Symptoms

Generalized Anxiety ("GAD")
A free-floating anxiety state that fills the sufferer with chronic worry, feelings of mounting tension and impending overwhelm - and is not attributed to any particular source. Remember, fears that revolve around a specific action or object are phobias – avoid the Feared Thing and anxiety is under control. With Generalized Anxiety, there doesn't seem to be anything the person can reliably do (or not do) to eliminate the agitation and fear.

Panic Attacks are accompanied by physical sensations – the body's response to a sudden burst of adrenaline. Generalized anxiety sufferers may not have trembling hands or shortness of breath. Instead, obsessive worry may be purely cognitive (intellectual/mental) and offer no visible physical signs of fear. As a disorder, the term is usually shortened to its initials and called "GAD".

Acute Stress & Post-Traumatic Stress
Extreme anxiety states that were originally provoked by trauma, violence, natural disaster, etc. The sufferer relives the emotional content of the bad event, often flashing back on remembered images and sounds. Can include vivid nightmares and a fear of sleep. People also report an emotional deadening of perceptions and feel like they're walking in a dream, or no longer able to feel connected to their own body. The terror is specifically tied to a traumatic event, but may over time, spread into a generalized anxiety state.

Symptoms

Disturbances of Mood

Depression
There is a broad spectrum to mood disorder symptoms. Many have strong connections to brain chemistry and hormonal production, while the source of others remains unclear. Depressive symptoms appear in a variety of forms, and often involve related anxiety states. Everyone has various moods and under certain circumstances, anyone can feel depressed. But blue moods are usually short-lived and have little impact on overall functioning.

*Clinical **Depression*** includes chronic and/or overwhelming feelings of:
    Hopelessness;
    Apathy/lack of emotional investment;
    Anxious rumination;
    Feelings of self-loathing;
    Social withdrawal, isolation;
    Chronic self-criticism

    Many depressive states are based on a crippling sadness that may be chronic (therefore limiting all functioning) or sporadic (which bring daily activities to a sudden halt). A person suffering chronic depression may have difficulty doing much beyond the barest survival tasks. Someone with episodic depression may attempt much more, but repeatedly and suddenly abandon all efforts and withdraw into a negative state as the mood plummets. That start/stop quality of life can eventually make any goal seem too overwhelming to start. People suffering from recurrent depressions are unable to count on their abilities to sustain energy and interest long enough to see any project to completion. Instead, it seem their lives are completely at the mercy of fluctuating moods.

| Symptoms |

Still other depressive states revolve around *detachment from identity/loss of sense of self*:
- Persistent emotional deadness; inability to *reach* one's own feelings while seeming to observe them from a distance.
- A recurring sense that one's human core is disappearing,
- While performing the motions of a daily life, one feels so remote from one's own *self* that actions have little meaning;
- Feelings of unreality that are increasingly disturbing.

These symptoms can be devastating – and I strongly urge anyone suffering to seek medical help. Anti-depressant medications can serve as a springboard to an entirely new mental state. While psychiatric drugs are not magic, they can be *very* successful in treating depression.

Deep depressive states are ego-syntonic – the patient cannot distinguish between a mental distortion and an accurate assessment of their own future. They think it's logical to feel so bad.

This is where mood disorders become dangerous – believing that the darkness one feels is an accurate picture of reality encourages thoughts about "giving up." In truth, illness is *creating* the darkness.

These distortions invoke a kind of emotional amnesia that prevents the sufferers from being able to remember ever feeling better. They literally cannot believe their mental state ever felt different or ever will feel different than it does at the moment.

ANY READER experiencing such feelings/thoughts should find a professional to talk with – from the depths of severe depression, your assessment of reality is incorrect. Do not trust it.

| Symptoms |

Agitated depression describes an anxiety state that is masking an underlying depression – while beneath that, the depression may be covering a different emotion such as rage. Depressive feelings are not sourced in apathy – usually very intense emotions are at its center. Hopelessness and lack of energy can be the result of anger that is redirected at the self. Depression is often considered "rage-turned-inward". That complex re-routing of feelings may appear as a state of chronic anxiety.

Likewise, a mood disturbance may be lurking beneath other symptoms. A depressive state might be covering up underlying anxiety. The point is: one overt symptom may be used to ward off a different set of feelings that are judged too threatening to be experienced directly. No easy answers – and impossible to self-diagnose from books.

Dysthymia: chronic unhappiness or persistent state of apathy. Inability to take any pleasure from living. Sometimes a patient will experience dysthymia for years (or a lifetime) and not recognize it as a symptom.

Major Depression: a chronic state of sadness or hopelessness of great intensity. The patient frequently lapses into deeper states of despair, losing all interest in life and including thoughts of suicide. Psychiatrists usually try medication immediately to provide a safety net for the severely depressed patient.

Emotional Volatility or Mood Swings are the hallmark of Bi-Polar Disorder, which is the newer term for Manic/Depressive illness. Most psychiatrists recognize a bio-chemical component in this disorder, and patients can be helped significantly with the right medication. But having manic moments alternating with low dips in mood is not the same thing as being Bi-Polar. Clinical *"mania"* is unlike any symptom most of us will ever experience. It is very different from anxious rumination, hyperactive energy, creative binges, or angry outbursts.

Wildly fluctuating emotions are common after-shocks of a breakdown. I felt like my emotional dam had broken, and I was experiencing everything in mythic proportions. On a given day, I could be enraged, petrified, ecstatic and despairing. The people around me seemed to be on a different plane of existence – they were living in a situation comedy, while I existed in a tragic opera.

Mood swings may be the result of other symptoms – feeling "high one day and low the next" does not mean you have a neuro-chemical problem. Many anxiety sufferers develop intense mood shifts – when not terrified, they are almost "high" - only to plummet back into hopelessness with the next panic attack. As you describe mood swings to a doctor, be specific regarding the *how* and *why* of your experience. Clarify whether a feeling state is new or has been a lifelong trait. Also include any particular events or thoughts that seem to precipitate an emotional leap.

On the other hand, if you suspect you do have bi-polar symptoms, mention it early in consultation. Certain medications interact poorly with the neuro-chemistry of that disorder, and a doctor should be made aware of the possibility.

Symptoms

Disturbances in Thought

Cerebral Panic:

I used this phrase to describe my worst anxiety states. Without warning, words would start running in my mind as if I had no control over them. They were specific patterns, phrases that repeated over and over. Eventually they seemed necessary – and I intentionally tried to keep thinking them, feeling something horrible would happen to my mind if I stopped. I was afraid to confess this one because it seemed like "hearing voices." And I was not hearing a delusion, but felt compelled to *think* one - all the while knowing it was fantasy. I was obsessed with observing every thought as if my own ideas could potentially do something *to* me. Lying down, trying to fall asleep, thoughts came as vividly as events in a dream. I was fully awake, but the language portion of a dream had started and that the thoughts in my own mind seemed not to belong to me.

Panic Attacks have a strong *physical* component – racing heart, shortness of breath, dizziness or other sensory responses. But a state of cerebral panic brought no physical changes. My heart rate stayed steady and moderate. No shortness of breath, no trembling hands. I was utterly petrified, yet I looked and sounded calm. For years, I would glance into mirrors to double and quadruple check for any outward signs of the racing fear inside my head. Nothing. I looked completely normal – which was almost more terrifying. How could such a discrepancy exist between the inside and outside of a mind? Sometimes I felt compelled to silently repeat my name, trying to hold onto a feeling of being alive or real. I *had* to keep thinking, but at the same time, I felt like my thoughts were trying to take over. **It was a non-stop battle for sovereignty over my own mind. Nothing worked, but I was consumed by the drive to stay hyper-vigilant.** The monologue was my anchor. To lose it would mean drifting off forever. I *needed* to keep thinking - in order to not disappear.

> **Symptoms**

Two Channels At Once

I walk down the street with a dear friend, and we talk about finding someplace to eat dinner. All day I have seemed normal, and at times, almost felt like a regular person. But any new idea, any new place to go or experience to endure is a potential trigger. Suddenly we are close to the restaurant... how did we get here so fast? It can't be right, something feels odd...it seemed we were walking in a different direction and suddenly ended up here. One challenge to my sense of reality - and the nightmare begins.

Carol holds the door and I walk in - I've agreed that yes, this is a good place to eat – I've approved it, I have...tried to remember how it looks and what could feel dangerous about being there. But there is never any way to tell, no way to prepare; I only pretend there are things I can do to make it easier. A waiter moves past us and there – out of nowhere – the rustle of someone's movements and the world is tilting.

Sure this table looks fine, I smile. And I slide onto a chair, or someone does...some flesh, some piece of human body that moves like me, that felt like me once...years ago. I can't do this; I'd been feeling strange, we should have picked someplace with softer lights. I won't be able to sit there, it has to be close to a door....not too crowded or too empty, nothing surreal, not seating that makes things look odd...but we're here. It's too late to think of what I might have said....and then it's as if I am still back on the sidewalk, walking with Carol. We are nowhere and everywhere – in dreams that happens. A thought moves flesh and blood. I am dreaming and can't wake up....

I can see the windows, watch the door...but there's too much noise, too many voices all going at once...she talks, my friend, and I smile and listen – but under her words, the other track is taking over... I tell her it's warm in here, already rehearsing lies... being prepared for what could come...stop it, stop doing this to your own mind....stop thinking! But this could really be the night it happens...nothing has ever looked so odd this *fast. A bad thought and efforts to stop it, okay, okay...I am okay so far.. no one has noticed, Carol seems okay, can't tell...and I'm centered, but my friend of ten years, her name sounds odd..a crazy thought, an untellable thought. I repeat my own name, I'm okay, okay..I'm here, it's real. But in the next second, my hands look strange, the lights are too bluish and the skin feels wrong...we laugh at something she says, it's all right to laugh, can be centering, I'm not bad tonight, this is not so bad...and I want to reach for the menu, anticipate it, then start to shift, knowing I need to move my right hand but it feels too distant...my fingers on the paper are wrong, as if deadened. It's okay, it's just the menu. I'm in the restaurant and it's only a menu. But it's not the same menu they used to have....or might be. Something is wrong with it. Something is very very wrong. I say words to Carol without really hearing what she asked. She knows. She must. Someone can tell. Don't think that, can't think that....no, I'm Janine. Janine Baker. Just Janine Baker, and I live on 97th Street. And it's a menu and my hands are all right.*

This has all been dreaming, not happening. I'm in one of the nightmares, but can't tell for sure... desperately look around for "normal things" – it can't be a dream if everything is normal, no dream creatures, no magical happenings...but Carol looks different, since she laughed just now, something changed...waiter brings water and I don't know if it's better or worse to drink...to calm down, or if the ice will feel strange...my lips aren't right, this is a dream...it's Dante. Not heaven or earth, can't be.... It's possible I have died, already died - and this is the moment that Something will tell me I'm not real anymore...carol asks a question and remarkably I answer, but...

I think I might step outside a minute, just got hot, a little too warm and she says I should drink some water, and I wonder if that is the signal for the nightmare to change....

Those are crazy thoughts, this is not true, not a dream, and I panic more when I make no sense...not making sense, not thinking right. This is it. This is the night it happens.

I step outside, and stand there trying to find something that doesn't look crazy...can't lose control, losing mySelf...I can't *go back in there, I can't sit through a meal. But I'll try, I have to. I can't – and I have to. For ten minutes I stand there and gather myself back in, try to pack my Self into this body, try to keep pretending. I am not of this earth. I was not meant to live in a human body...scanning the window to see if Carol is okay, still sitting there, she'll wait, I can make myself go back...will say it was too hot...no one hears this, no one knows this. Can't know, must not know.... Don't <u>tell</u> me I am not insane!*

This night is not unusual. It's the way I've gotten used to living.

Victims of a serious accident are usually encouraged to keep talking during a rescue – to maintain consciousness by staying connected to people around them. They might describe their environment, or recite their name, address or phone number. That is how I felt as I repeated my own name or was compelled to silently identify objects in view (*"this is the chair, I'm right here in the restaurant, I can see the chair, I'm okay, this is the chair..."*). I felt in danger of slipping outside my own awareness – and needed to keep reminding myself where and even who I was.

Symptoms

Disturbances in Thought

Obsessions, Compulsions & Magical Thinking

Hypochondria

This term is often used incorrectly to describe someone who *pretends* to be sick and invents symptoms. In truth, people who suffer hypochondria are <u>completely sincere</u> in their conviction that something is wrong inside their bodies. Far from inventing complaints to get attention, they are so scared of illness (and pending death) they often minimize the severity of symptoms when talking to a doctor in an effort to postpone hearing the "bad news". As a diagnosis, the term indicates someone who is convinced (a) they have something seriously physically wrong– disease, illness, injury – and despite medical evidence to the contrary, cannot be reassured of their own health; or b) are obsessed with the idea that they *will* develop an illness and must constantly be on the lookout for symptoms.

Many anxiety sufferers hyper-focus on the body, if not before the breakdown, at least as a result. We worry about our heart rate and check it frequently. We monitor our own breathing, our ability to swallow, and every ping and pang felt during a day. Always on the alert for *"what's wrong now?"* we become overly-attuned to the fluid human body – convinced that something critical will be missed.

It is a pattern that feeds on itself. **Fear is reinforced by chronic self-monitoring, not eliminated.** The more closely we focus on every physical nuance, the better we get at noticing change. That soon gives us a wider range of potential illnesses to dread, followed by more indignation from feeling misunderstood. In its severe form, the sufferer goes from doctor to doctor, then hospital to hospital, convinced the illness is not taken seriously by any professional.

Symptoms

Disturbances in Thought

Full-blown Hypochondria is an example of a symptom becoming syntonic with a patient's ego. The patient does not ask *"what's wrong with me that makes me believe I have some disease?"* Instead they lament *"what's wrong with the doctors that that they can't find it?!"* They are unable to see that the real symptom is their False Belief.

Ruminating on Mental Symptoms & the Development of Obsessive Introspection

A similar problem can develop in relation to *psychiatric* symptoms. Struggling to recover, we are tempted to take our own emotional temperature on an hourly basis (or in my own case, more frequently than *that*).

"Do I feel better or worse than I did last night?" "Am I more anxious after taking a walk, or am I a little calmer now, or... I might have been calmer when I first woke up, but now after eating something... that spaciness is getting worse again."

An express ticket to deeper misery. I cannot emphasize this enough – **fight the urge to monitor every feeling**. It may seem sensible and self-care taking, but that's an illusion. You will only train yourself to notice the most subtle nuances – and already highly anxious, you will overvalue their significance. Try to realize that you are stuck in a mild form of paranoia, and unable to accurately assess the meaning of every detail you notice.

A highly skilled detective misses very few clues. But a highly skilled *paranoid* detective will have a life of misery. Everything in sight becomes crucial evidence, potential proof – even when there is no crime to investigate.

> **Symptoms**

Obsessions

Recurring thoughts, ideas or images that persist in the mind despite great efforts to dismiss them. Also includes irrational fears centering around certain ideas – a patient may attach "meaning" to their recurring thoughts as if being warned of disaster and must focus even harder to counteract the imagined dangers.
These symptoms are usually reported as ego-alien – *"Of course I know it's ridiculous to keep thinking this way, but I can't help it. It just takes me over."* In Obsessive Compulsive Disorder the sufferer spends incredible amounts of time and energy trying to ward off dangers with actions or rituals that bear no connection to the imagined disaster.

The High Cost of Magic

Magical Thinking

It struck me as remarkable that I felt terrified every single time I had a feeling of unreality. Shouldn't I deduce that it was the exact same sensation - had not harmed me the last twenty times - so why should it hurt me now? But despite logic, every episode was as frightening as the first.

Part of the explanation is that I was feeding the power of those symptoms every day by harboring bizarre fantasies. *What if this universe is really not at all what we believe it to be? What if in that altered state, my self is being transported off into some other dimension, into some way station between heaven and hell? What if madness is just too much insight into a Reality we're afraid to confront?*

So each time I started to feel peculiar, I easily jumped to *"this is it! This is finally the time my Self will vanish....I've tried to believe it was only anxiety, but I knew it was more, that it was something extraordinary.."* And with those magical beliefs egging me on, each episode mounted. I would never "get used to it" any more than a healthy person could be unfazed during a recurring nightmare. Believing in magical thoughts will prolong illness. Every time I let myself wonder if this world was real, or question if the Self could detach from its body, I set the stage for the next episode.

Ironically, right smack in the middle of an anxiety attack, I did my clearest thinking. While terrified, I clung hard to Logic and renounced all thoughts of unreality. It was only when I felt stronger and safer that I ventured back into bizarre territory. Fueled by a need to prove I wasn't afraid of such ideas, I felt empowered by exploring "crazy" thinking. That was justification for the same old obsessive patterns that, of course, reinforced the familiar cycle and set up the next attack. With mental symptoms, most roads lead right back to the same bad patterns.

Compulsions

A Compulsion is a *behavior* rather than a thought – might be a repeated ritual or "good luck" action that must be performed repeatedly and immediately. If resisted, anxiety levels rise until it becomes impossible to concentrate on anything except the action that must be performed.

This action must be done *now*– even though it could not realistically have any effect on the desired result.

"Just maybe…"
or
The Seductive 1%

In these thought patterns, the distinction between Syntonic and Dystonic can be very important. The patients, being sane, clearly recognize that the desperation around those rituals is absurd. They sincerely want to stop, and even more to the point, they want choice over their own actions. That sounds like an Ego-

Symptoms

alien symptom because the patients condemn their own actions – and wish to disown their obsessions.

But…somewhere in the recesses of mind, we are also capable of *believing* in the magic behind our compulsions. At some point in the process, we buy into the illusion that *just maybe* this ritual somehow protects me and my loved ones.

At that moment, the symptom is *syntonic* with the ego – and that is the moment that solidifies the illness. We both know and *don't* know that our magical thinking is irrational. We admit it inspires actions that accomplish nothing, but then harbor secret beliefs that "just maybe…" That is the proverbial nail in the coffin of recovery.

If prone to these symptoms, watch for the times you play both sides of the net – attempting to choose reality **and** magic, hedging your bets in a frightening universe … just in case.

That is precisely what I did for years – allowing the magical thinking to become syntonic with my self.

I was 99% clear that my disturbing obsessions were not logical. I was 99% sure that believing in magic was pure fantasy.

It was the remaining 1% that kept me ill.

It might seem that whatever we hold true the majority of the time should completely counteract any moments we spend playing along with distorted beliefs. But it's not a math problem. While 99% *should* outweigh a 1% lapse, it won't. And letting go of that last 1% can be the hardest change to make.

Some readers might be thinking: *But I've had harmless magical ideas all my life. I just need to keep it in perspective and then I can go back to how I was before this breakdown.* Wrong. The breakdown changed things – it was a wake-up call that now demands major adjustments in the way you deal with reality.

We realize that thoughts/fantasies stimulate emotions i.e., ruminating over a bizarre idea creates anxiety, laboring in a sad memory can summon depression. But that process also works in reverse. Strong emotions inspire thoughts to express them. We have many intense feelings, sourced by thoughts outside awareness. Consciously, we invent reasons for those feelings – looking around for evidence to support how we feel at a given moment.

The fantasies that we create are *products* of overwhelming emotions. The feelings came first – and the bizarre ideas are our invented explanations for why we feel so scared.

And it can get even sneakier. Sometimes the feeling itself is bypassed -- expressed only by the fantasy that symbolizes it. Unaware of being anxious at all, we substitute a bizarre compulsion to represent our fear. As long we perform a certain action that we feel compelled to perform, we remain unaware of our anxiety. In truth, powerful fear is *sourcing* the obsessive ritual and in time, one compulsion will turn into 20, then 50 and soon 100… No amount of actions can fully satisfy because they are only substitutes for a still unacknowledged fear.

You cannot control how you feel, but you <u>can</u> resist believing in the fantasies (delusions) that your emotions create. Anxiety can make us susceptible to outrageous ideas – don't let those ideas settle in and become part of you.

The same holds true for self-monitoring. We want to stop the constant rumination, yet we keep feeding it – as if the very act of harping on them is preventing bad things from happening. After all, we obsessed about it yesterday and nothing horrific occurred –

maybe those obsessions are necessary to keep us from getting worse. That us very dangerous territory for anyone trying to heal.

And of course, we know better. At least, we know to *say* we know better, which is a decent start. Just remember that your handful of good luck rituals and secret games give the mind a safe haven for disturbing thoughts. Pockets of delusional thinking that never see the light of reality are a breeding ground for increasingly strange ideas. While working to heal, choose reality at every opportunity. It is nearly impossible to fully recover while trying to straddle both sides of the fence.

Symptoms

Disturbances of Consciousness
Depersonalization and Derealization

I know that my self is vanishing, and soon all I will be is a body, a shell... every piece of me dead and gone.

When I think of Me (as if that creature ever existed)...it, she, I... belong in a different dimension, in another world from another time.

Symptoms may appear with the sudden sensation that you are existing in a dream. Everything looks odd, somehow "off", flat or two-dimensional. It happens instantly – almost with a jolt -- as if you have been transmitted into an alternate reality. (I know this sounds too bizarre to be in the realm of sanity – yet it is).

These are descriptions of **Depersonalization** and **Derealization** – disorienting states of consciousness that feel like a break with reality. But reality-testing is intact. The experience is usually described with the phrase 'as if' – *as if I'm not real; as if I am losing my mind* – while knowing those are imaginary distortions. These symptoms fall under the umbrella of **Dissociation** – altered states of consciousness, akin to trances.

(The term *dissociation* is also used in connection with Multiple Personality Disorder or "MPD" - now called Dissociative Identity Disorder or "DID". But that is a highly rare phenomenon and will not develop from long-term depersonalization or nervous breakdowns. MPD is not a condition that is addressed in this book).

Dissociation involves the splintering of different aspects of consciousness from the overall observing self, allowing them to co-exist without requiring integration into the larger picture. In the process, we recognize what is real while simultaneously distancing ourselves from its impact.

Depersonalization is a normal phenomenon of the human brain experienced under extreme conditions – ranging from violent accidents/traumas to the news of winning a huge lottery. At such times, people may report *"this feels like it's not really happening"* or *"It's as if I'm in a dream..."*

That split in consciousness comes from the mind's inability to integrate new facts/ideas into the picture of reality that was perceived true only seconds earlier. A sudden and drastic loss of status quo causes the mind to challenge the *literal reality* of such moments. By creating a delay in our absorption of the event, we are buying extra time (and perspective) before needing to incorporate a drastic change into our mental equilibrium. It is not a malfunction of the brain. Anyone with a proclivity for dissociation can enter such states of consciousness.

But it can be a sy*mptom* when occurring frequently or without external provocation.

| Symptoms |

Disturbances of Consciousness
Depersonalization and Derealization

*No one could understand. I am literally not here anymore...all the while some piece of me is still **observing** my non-existence. My brain has turned itself inside out.*

Depersonalization and **Derealization** can be petrifying experiences. I have devoted a chapter to these symptoms because information on them can be very hard to find. You are not the only person on earth to feel this way- and these states of mind are not indicative of damaged brains.

"My hands feel like paper...something artificial, not human..." "I am not hallucinating, but I can't recognize myself, it's like I've never really seen my own reflection before..." "I can't feel my body, not actually numb, but I'm NOT ME...like I'm disappearing within my Self..." "Sometimes I even wonder if I'm dead, a ghost...it's like my soul is trying to leave its body. I can't tell if I'm dreaming or awake..." "I must be going insane, to feel my Self wafting away...I know it's only a matter of time..."

Depersonalization is the disturbing experience of feeling disconnected from one's own body/self, often described as if living in a dream. It may involve the physical body alone, or include a loss of connection to personal identity/sense of self. The sufferers *feel* as if they literally do not exist while still being able to reason and assess reality. Depersonalization may begin as a detachment from bodily awareness and progress to an inability to feel fully awake. Increased anxiety can exacerbate these feelings because mounting fear is more impetus to withdraw from awareness. The result may be recurring anxiety attacks accompanied by delusions that the self is disintegrating.

Symptoms

"In a split second, the world seems to tilt...I don't recognize things in my own house as belonging there, nothing looks normal ..." "Reality has vanished, or is closing in...as if the literal edge of the world is right beyond the horizon..." "Everyone around me looks 'off' somehow, like they're robots, not people..it's as if I've never even SEEN members of my own family before..." "My neighborhood looks like a stage set or artificial replica of how it used to be.." "It's like I'm in a dream or have been given LSD..."

Derealization is often described as detachment from the environment, as if a plate of glass is between the self and the world. Objects and other people appear two-dimensional, or made of cardboard. These are not actual hallucinations, but are described "*as if*" everything appears somehow changed.

The ability to reality-test remains intact. Concentration requires great effort, and the harder the sufferer tries to focus on something external, the more disconnected from it they become. Often includes feelings of déjà vu or jamais vu. The most familiar places look increasingly bizarre, surreal – as if they belong in a Salvador Dali painting.

Both DP and DR involve similar states of consciousness. The distinction is that the first encompasses a distorted awareness of self, while the second refers to distorted feelings about one's **environment**. If a person is prone to one, they may frequently experience the other. From this point forward, I use "**DP/DR**" to indicated either or both.

These states of mind are usually accompanied by an obsessive need to self-monitor, to watch oneself living moment-by-moment. Soon, observation replaces living – sufferers report an inability to *experience* their own lives, and an unremitting compulsion to watch a self that seems to be vanishing.

| Symptoms |

It's not helpful to be told *"just stop thinking about it so much"* -- although you'll likely get that advice. These ideas are not the result of an intentional focusing; instead, we have become trapped by our own ruminations – as if we lost the channel changer to our cognitive television. It automatically selects the program of *obsession*, and we are forced to watch.

Usually, but not exclusively, DP/DR will be accompanied by overwhelming fears of losing complete contact with reality. We might believe that we are literally willing ourselves to stay sane. We might alternate between a morbid *fear of* and inexplicable *desire to give in* to what feels like an inevitable psychosis. This conflict between the opposing desires of resistance and surrender will increase anxiety and feed the compulsion to keep a vigilant watch over oneself. Such thoughts can become the activities of the day – with time taking on a surreal meaning. Events occurring in reality can pale when compared to the intense and rapid exercises inside the mind. And detachment increases.

All we want is to live in the real world again. Yet what we *do* is fall deeper into self-monitoring and what could have been a short-lived dissociative moment solidifies into an altered state of mind that lasts day after day. Fear/anxiety leads to increased self-awareness which reinforces the DP/DR -- until you feel lost in a puzzle of your own inverted consciousness – aware of too much *inside* your mind, and increasingly detached from anything residing outside it.

It seems preposterous to suggest this could be caused by nothing but thoughts. Reality itself is being played with -- and you grow certain there must be neurological damage behind it.

Symptoms

Disturbances of Consciousness
Depersonalization and Derealization

Sometimes episodes of DP/DR begin after recreational drug use, leading sufferers to believe they have destroyed some brain cells. More likely, the altered drug state opened a window to highly disturbing thoughts (ones completely contrary to the reality we always thought we knew) and the status quo of the very self seemed at jeopardy.

Extremely disturbing thoughts can also be a provocation for DP/DR without any form of drug use. An idea or thought assaults the defenses of "who we are" to such a massive degree that the integrity of identity is challenged. Having nowhere to run, if the mind separates itself into fragments of awareness – splintering feelings from thoughts -- and thoughts from memories -- and memories from emotions -- and emotions from perceptions.

A conundrum remains–
- It feels like a break with reality;
  - But cognitive functioning is retained.

The solution caused a split between conflicting areas of consciousness.

In the process, what gets lost is the experience of our own perception to know what's Real (the actual perception isn't lost – just the Experience of *owning* the perception). Suddenly we are in a state of both knowing and not knowing at the same time.

We know who we are, where we are and what is real, but it feels as if we don't know – yet at the same time, we are fully aware that we accurately do. If you suffer from DP/DR, I am sure these descriptions speak to you. If you have not experienced it, this whole chapter probably seems more bizarre than informative.

MODES OF ALTERED CONSCIOUSNESS IN DEPERSONALIZATION STATES™®
©Janine Baker, 2003

- *Obsessive Thoughts*
- *Sensory Distortions*
- *Memory Disturbance*
- *Emotional Deadness*
- *Loss of Identity or Authenticity*

The statements below describe perceptions/disturbances that fall under the Depersonalization umbrella. Following those, 5 modes of consciousness correspond to the different ways DP can be expressed.

First, make a checkmark next to any statement you consider true for you. (For now, disregard the letters to the left).

A   Have frequent bizarre thoughts that almost seem plausible such as "what if I am imagining the entire world?" or "what if I am asleep right now & only dreaming my experience?"

A   Often disturbed by your vivid imagination & unusual ideas.

A   Attracted to (and frightened by) questions about human existence, infinity, meanings of reality.

A   Preoccupied by fears of death.

B   Periodically focus on automatic bodily actions such as breathing, swallowing, speaking or seeing to the extent that you feel you must concentrate in order to keep it functioning.

B   Often feel as if parts of your body are not really there, or somehow are not familiar.

B   Feeling that you need to will your Self to stay within the perimeters of your own body.

B   Certain lighting triggers intense feelings of unreality or disconnection from your own body (especially fluorescents -- such as department store overhead lights).

C   Able to recall specific personal experiences, but often feel as if they happened to someone else.

C   Feel there is something seriously wrong with your memory & ability to process information.

C   Have difficulty perceiving when events occurred (as if yesterday is very far off, while memories from years ago feel fresh).

C   Have great difficulty with activities that require concentration and directed focus such as reading, writing, providing detailed explanations, etc.

D   Able to feel appropriately deep emotions in response to characters in movies or stories, but unable to access your own feelings during real interactions in day-to-day life.

D   Possess a conviction that you are too "numb" to really be hurt by anyone.

D   While knowing what you should or would feel, a sense of experiencing your own emotions is unavailable.

D   Often doubt your ability to feel love.

E   Frequently (& intentionally) imagine being someone else, or spend time acting as if you are a different person.

E   Convinced you're always wearing a façade (or social mask) that presents a very different picture from what lies underneath (even before the breakdown).

E   Vacillate between (a) thinking that you have superior knowledge, talents or insights; and (b) sudden intense feelings that you might not exist at all.

E   Films like "*The Matrix*", "*The Sixth Sense*", and "*Being John Malkovich*" strike a deep and lingering fear in you.

> **MODES OF ALTERED CONSCIOUSNESS IN DEPERSONALIZATION STATES™®**
>
> - *Obsessive Thoughts*
> - *Sensory Distortions*
> - *Memory Disturbance*
> - *Emotional Deadness*
> - *Loss of Identity or Authenticity*

The letters to the left of each question refer to <u>five different modes of consciousness</u>. If you have a majority of "A" responses, your DP/DR is primarily experienced as disturbances of Thought & Rumination. The letters correspond as follows:

A = Thoughts/Ruminations
B = Sensory/Perceptions
C = Attention/Memory
D = Emotional Accessibility
E = Sense of Identity/Authenticity

Thoughts/Ruminations: obsessive questioning, self-monitoring of one's own thoughts; mounting doubts about a universal reality, confusion over dream states versus waking, chronic ruminations about death, infinity, afterlife. Compulsion towards finding an acceptable Answer for every uncertainty and an inability to dismiss questions as beyond anyone's grasp. Like the constant picking at a scab, this rumination prevents stronger aspects of oneself from healing over – and the habit/obsession will create more anxiety which in turn will create more obsessing.

Sensory/Perceptions: disturbances in the perception of your body in space (feeling taller, shorter, too far, too close, etc. to what you intellectually perceive in reality). Chronic concern with the inability to feel oriented. Any disturbances involving the senses – obsessions that things don't look right or feel right – anxiety over touching objects that don't seem to be made of the right material – or feelings of one's own flesh being artificial.

MODES OF ALTERED CONSCIOUSNESS IN DEPERSONALIZATION STATES™®

- *Obsessive Thoughts*
- *Sensory Distortions*
- *Memory Disturbance*
- *Emotional Deadness*
- *Loss of Identity or Authenticity*

Attention/Memory: Difficulty concentrating, especially attempting to focus at will. When reading, words don't seem to sink in and one may turn the page only to realize he has no idea what words he just read. Actual memory is intact, but the feeling of how long ago something happened is distorted. Activities requiring quick thinking are frightening (and often avoided) because at the first failure, one jumps to fears of being brain-damaged, having a pre-mature form of senility or Alzheimer's disease. The result is a conviction that one's intellect is about half what it once was.

Emotional Accessibility: Inability to experience emotional response while retaining knowledge of how you would feel if you could reach your own emotions. A constant longing to be within one's own feelings instead of observing them from a distance. Sensation of being the camera person rather than the actor – always from the vantage point of watching and not being part of the scene.

Sense of Identity/Authenticity: Disturbances in ability to perceive one's self (the you inside your own mind as opposed to you, the physical body). Knowledge remains, but the experience is as if you are no longer yourself, or never existed. This is different from the physical distortions such as feeling one's hand is made of a foreign substance, or that one's body is floating or fading. Identity disturbances can increase to the point of truly feeling as if the very "I" of the self has disintegrated – living without a soul, without a core person, one feels destined to exist on some inexplicable plane as a body that no longer houses a person. The only remaining feeling is abject terror of isolation – and it is chronic.

MODES OF ALTERED CONSCIOUSNESS IN DEPERSONALIZATION STATES™®

- *Obsessive Thoughts*
- *Sensory Distortions*
- *Memory Disturbance*
- *Emotional Deadness*
- *Loss of Identity or Authenticity*

Intense DP episodes consume the *entire* body/self/mind, leaving no place to go for momentary relief or distraction. But efforts to escape it create a paradox – actively trying to avoid self-awareness usually makes dissociation worse.

Sometimes I could find relief after breaking my DP experiences into specific areas of consciousness/perception. I needed to tease apart which areas felt most distorted at a given time and which seemed relatively untouched. It gave me focus, and more importantly, gave me at least a modicum of control over where I *placed* my focus. Otherwise, it was like being a passive traveler on an acid trip.

My worst fears were experienced within Mode 2 (Sensory/Perception Distortions) If I let myself focus on my body during an escalating episode, I could reach states of panic. Relaxation techniques can work well for generalized anxiety, but they might backfire with depersonalization symptoms. Mediation and visualization exercises were disastrous for me – they required concentrating on the reality of the body, its boundaries, properties, breathing, skin sensations, etc. with the objective of centering or reconnecting to the real moment to dispel imaginary fears. But regardless of logical thinking, my anxiety levels intensified from even the slightest attention to my own body, skin, motor responses or breathing. Guided thoughts such as *"this is my flesh regardless of how I feel"* and *"it's only a sensation and cannot harm me"* might make dp/dr sufferers feel worse. If you are especially troubled by DP sensations under Mode 2, be cautious with any techniques that *enhance* awareness of your body

Redirect focus *away* from your dominant area of distortion.

My intellect functioned pretty well even during anxious states, and when the dp/dr was especially bad, I found distraction in the area of *Attention/Memory*. For me, logic and linear thinking never increased feelings of unreality. So it became a safe mode - I knew I could read non-fiction articles, work word puzzles, or simple arithmetic problems to try without deepening my bizarre feelings. Reading material needed to be very *dry* – nothing that might stimulate imagination. The key was to focus on a subject that demanded a *cognitive workout* without invoking strong emotions.

Someone else will find the exact opposite to be true – feeling an *increased* anxiety within Attention/Memory modes. ("*I can't remember things – can't concentrate. Something is wrong with my brain...*") In that case, put emphasis *on* bodily awareness (Sensory/Perceptions) -- activities such as exercise, dance, stretching, whatever enhances physical sensation. It need not be exertion – even long hot baths, massage, cooking/tasting, brushing one's hair – actions that put the spotlight on *bodily self* without demanding linear thinking.

Focusing *directly* on our most troubling areas of unreality will *deepen* the experience. *Elsewhere. Other. Outward.* Keep the focus away from your perceived distortion.

Depersonalization as secondary to: Anxiety or Depression

Although psychiatry recognizes Depersonalization *Disorder*, DP is usually experienced *secondary* to another symptom or disorder. Most DP/DR states seem to be caused by underlying anxiety or depression, and doctors begin by targeting one of those symptoms.

Regarding the categories in the Modes of Consciousness questionnaire: I suspect that when depersonalization is experienced mostly as *Obsessive Thoughts* or *Sensory Disturbances* it indicates an anxiety base. Likewise, depersonalization showing up primarily as *Memory Disturbances* or *Emotional Deadness* is likely based in depression. However, the ideas presented in this section (*Modes of Consciousness*) are entirely my own, and not part of any diagnostic process or assessment. They are based only on personal experiences and those described to me by other sufferers.

Anxiety-based DP – probably dominated by:
Obsessive Thoughts;
Sensory Disturbances

Depression-based DP – probably dominated by:
Memory Disturbances;
Emotional Deadness

Identity Disturbance appears equally in both, and is the very hallmark of dissociation. It is also the most common way to describe DP/DR - *"I feel unreal"* or *"I can't connect to feeling like myself."* Those are decent descriptions, but rather general. Try to distinguish your personal brand of DP – i.e, how the state of mind makes you *feel* as well as how it appears. It will help the doctor determine its underlying cause.

Extreme Unreality

Frightening Lights

Fluorescents can turn an ordinary room into a David Lynch movie. Surreal, ominous, otherworldly. I functioned better on a lonely New York street late at night (where any normal person would be scared) than I did on an afternoon trip to Walmart.

Large department stores, small offices with no windows, classrooms, seminar halls – any place with those garish blue/white lights – lights that cast no shadows and seem to outline objects and people in a supernatural aura. The effect is dreamlike – and we can momentarily believe that we *are* dreaming, that there is no longer an outside reality and we're just "seeing" everything as projections of our own imaginations.

Powerful responses to blue spectrum lighting are commonly reported among DP/DR sufferers, with increased anxiety and obsessions of identity loss or sudden disappearance of self.

Unreal "others"

This distortion can be uniquely disturbing. One day the people around you no longer look "*right*". Although recognizable, identifiable – somehow they are not themselves. It can feel as if the face you observe is a replica or "*double*" of someone who is playing the role of the real person.

Or you might perceive other people as not being human, but machine-like… all you can think about are the inner workings of their brain's mechanics, without being able to notice their human qualities. Interestingly, the more familiar the face, the less normal it may look. A casual acquaintance might appear only *mildly* different, and their faces will not cause as much anxiety as the sudden appearance of a loved one who no longer seems familiar.

As you talk with people, you cannot focus on the content of their words, but only on how their brains must be functioning - you try to picture the neurons and chemicals that make the mouth move, or send signals to make the face laugh or frown. The result is a total dehumanization of the other person – and of yourself by extension. You are left noticing nothing but the trees -- the details alone – with no ability to appreciate a forest. It makes genuine connection to others seem nearly impossible.

In this experience, your mind has taken the distortions that once only applied to your *self* and thrown them over everyone around you. No one else is real either. Never were. You have invented the entire universe as if it is one long night dream. Do not even try to explain this one to family and friends. They will never get it, and you might scare them witless.

Can I Ever Feel Real Again?

Absolutely. Keep connections with other people. Talk, and keep talking – even when you feel artificial. And here is the hardest part...try to stop focusing on how you feel. Persistent efforts to understand our bizarre states of mind only force us to tune in deeper and closer. At this point, the mind needs to function without being watched like a hawk.

Finding the perfect description for your mind state is not going to help you heal. Focusing *elsewhere* is the key.

The solution requires distracting yourself long enough to let your consciousness re-weave a sense of identity. But you can't force that process.

You need to move aside and allow your mind to repair itself.

Remember that nothing has actually happened to your brain. Something has gone wrong in your ability to *consciously perceive* an on-going sense of identity. But your identity is still there. Your personality, all your memories, likes/dislikes – all aspects of *you* are intact.

In DP/DR states, the temporary ability to *consciously experience self* has gone haywire. If the television cable fails, reception is thwarted, but nothing is wrong at the studio where the show is being filmed. And in states of dissociation, nothing is wrong with the cognitive faculties that process information. Only the connection (your conscious temporary perception) is askew.

One tip cannot be emphasized enough – keep your gaze **outward.**

Talk to people. Stay involved in life. Go out. Walk. See different things. Have coffee in a diner. Go to the mall. Read the mail. Buy the paper. Call a friend. See a movie. Keep living.

You may feel like a complete robot, but even without one authentic bone in you – fake it. Keep moving, keep focusing outward – with every inch of your being.

You cannot lift out of this nightmare by focusing harder on how the dissociation feels. It seems like you can – you will feel possessed by the need to just *figure it all out* or to delve even deeper and think harder in search of profound insights about reality or the nature of consciousness. All lies. Delusions of the symptom.

Focus *outward*.

Picking Up The Pieces

The Kind of Person Who Comes Unraveled

A breakdown may come as complete shock:
*"How on earth could something like this be happening to **me**?!"*
There may be little or no warning, beginning as a panic attack during on ordinary day while performing ordinary tasks. Or emotional outbursts and overwhelming dark feelings may enter from nowhere.
    These are the experiences of people who never considered the possibility of a breakdown, and feel utterly betrayed by their own minds.

    For others, it may be less shock than disappointment. Some people remember very rough spots in the past – with a hint of symptoms here or there. But somehow through sheer will power, they kept pushing through bad feelings and fears, and finally believed it was behind them.
    "But I had everything under control."

    Then others of us were barely holding on for years. Although we might claim not to have seen this coming, deep down we think:
    'I knew it was just a matter of time."

    It can be reassuring to recognize one of those descriptions, or you may begin worrying that 1) having a breakdown out of nowhere; or 2) after a failed attempt at handling problems; or 3) as some inevitable collapse [whichever is your own] has a much worse prognosis, will be harder to treat, or *means something* more horrible than the other two. Utterly unfounded, and just more fuel for obsessions.

    Breakdowns come in many flavors and they occur in people with a variety of histories. Recovery is recovery. Watch for the temptation to scare yourself by jumping to worst case scenarios – believing that a secret in your history will make *your* recovery impossible. Those worries and false hunches quickly turn into ground of being. Consistent ruminating is a luxury you cannot afford right now. It will take on a life of its own, and trying to reverse it is much harder than preventing it before it takes hold. Start noticing how often you reach for the worst possible fantasy outcome. And do everything you can to stop this habit in its tracks.

    Be on special alert for dark thoughts connected to magical beliefs. Example: *if I imagine the worst, that will keep anything bad from really happening.* It can actually feel like you are doing something constructive/protective by torturing yourself with the most awful things your mind can conjure, as if the act of worrying serves as a magic charm to ward off disaster. In reality those ideas are preposterous – and nurturing them is a form of omnipotent delusion. Feeling utterly helpless, you try to over-compensate by believing in fantastic ideas to briefly make you feel powerful. It is an *illusion* of control that offers nothing except deeper misery. That kind of fantasy itself is a symptom. Do not keep giving into it.

Not a Trauma In Sight

Sometimes a mind comes unraveled as the result of a traumatic event (victim of assault, violent accident, major illness, etc.). But there need not be an obvious disaster. In fact, life may have been going pretty well before your onset of symptoms – you might have been on the verge of new opportunities, relationships, growth experiences. And that adds to the bewilderment – *why now? Nothing was wrong*!

Trauma comes in many forms. It may not be visibly shocking or occur around terrible events. Psychological trauma can be the result of any sudden or profound rupture to one's **status quo** (our sense of inner balance and control), because symptoms are triggered by thoughts, not events. The mind can interpret something as highly *traumatic* that goes unnoticed by any observer.

This bears repeating: **symptoms are triggered by *thoughts*, not events.** That is a hard concept to grasp, especially while in the midst of bizarre sensations that seem unrelated to any particular thought or idea. And if we imagine being traumatized by a disaster or violent act, it seems logical to interpret any future symptom as a direct result of that *event*. But in truth, such symptoms would be the result of our *thoughts* about that event, our "take" on it, our response to it, and the resulting disruption of our inner status quo. This may sound like hair-splitting, but it is a crucial distinction for understanding symptom formation and the possible origins of nervous breakdowns.

Transitions often act as catalysts for traumatic reactions. Junctions in life, cross roads (even pleasant ones) may activate doubts about who we are and how we see the world. In retrospect, it is common for sufferers to realize their breakdowns were timed around one of the following:
- The first year at college;
- Shortly after moving to a new location;
- After the breakup of a relationship
- When forming a new relationship;
- Upon graduating school;

- After having a child.

Naturally those events bring higher stress merely because they demand adaptations. But something else is inherent in them – transitions mark a potential revision in how we see ourselves. Even if pleased with the new direction, we feel a threat – although it may not be felt on a conscious level. Something within self is at risk. Our old repertoire may not work in this new situation. *How to move forward without losing what I've already built? How to **intentionally** change – before massive changes happen to me? How to foreshadow internal changes rather than noticing them after the fact?* All questions that boil down to *how do I maintain my inner status quo*?

What held you together for 18 years may not be enough to sustain a move to adulthood. What worked in early relationships will not necessarily transfer to new ones. Although bad situations feel painfully familiar, it can feel even scarier to imagine suddenly living without them. *Change is a massive threat to our sense of control.*

Any version of believing *"now my life is really beginning – everything that went before this doesn't count!"* is a red flag that too much is being swept under your proverbial mental rug. Intense efforts to wipe the past away, belittle it, discount it, etc. can set the stage for symptoms during a life transition.

Constant Fears of the Unknown

From the time I was a child, I was haunted by certain ideas. When they dominated my mind I was terrified, and at times they mysteriously receded. But I couldn't even enjoy the peace, because I needed to try to predict when they might return. Whether present or hidden, the thoughts were with me, and threatening to cloak any moment in blackness.

To this day, I am amazed that anyone else could possibly think these things. These Thoughts were *my* secret hell. They belonged to me. They ruined my life.

Death;
The Supernatural;
Insanity;
Vanishing into thin air;
Entering another dimension;
Dismemberment; pieces of a body separating;
The isolation of outer space;
Being buried alive, unable to speak or move;
   Being unconscious/Being under anesthesia but
   able to hear and feel;
Infinity;
Self before birth/Self after death.

Normal people knew those concepts – but they ignored them. They changed the channel. They turned away. While I ran towards them.

At 14, I became obsessed with the idea of something horrible happening to me, and most importantly, that it could happen at any moment. I remember sitting in a classroom and suddenly imagining my heart "giving out." One thought, one idea crossing my mind or an ordinary day. One thought that seemed to open a portal to terror.

I started checking my pulse after walking up stairs or eating – and then after walking at all. I periodically checked it while sitting still – just to be sure it wasn't too fast *or* too *slow*. When I woke up in the morning, the first thing I did was feel my heartbeat.

During the day, I pushed my finger against my neck a dozen times an hour – casually feeling for the heartbeat without bringing any attention to myself. I was good at it, very subtle. I could appear interested in something else while counting. I needed to be sure it was still working – and that is was not too strong or too weak...steady. Alive.

And that was the first of the Thoughts that I decided to keep secret – I was constantly checking for verification that I was still alive.

Lying in bed, riding the bus, walking to school, I had to imagine how it might feel to die. The sensation of slipping away, or beginning to enter a state of non-being. How might it feel...to know ahead of time how it might feel.

I was trying to prepare – or *practice* – for the inevitable ultimate experience. I *needed* to *know* ahead of time how frightening the confusion could be, leaving self, leaving reality and entering a world never seen from this one. I *needed to know **how*** terrifying and in exactly what ways it would feel bewildering – desperate to imagine the unimaginable in the name of lessening the shock.

And I thought of *"forever"* and infinity...more and more and then more...and...more still...incomprehensible endlessness, but even with that, more...and more still.

No other thoughts could compete with obsessions about oblivion and eternity. Trying to wrap my mind around concepts that were beyond comprehension - yet aware that they could not be comprehended... it was unreachable – it was oblivion; it was infinity – more unknown than known. And more still.

"Beyond comprehension" – the phrase itself was unbearable, but at the same time, impossible to dismiss. To forget such words seemed the greatest danger. Never let the guard down, do not forget, do not look away...the phrases "when no one's looking" and "in the blink of an eye" were terrifying. *There is nothing wrong with me – I'm only playing, only thinking. Some people are just deep thinkers.*

I needed to somehow find ways of turning impossible thoughts into something manageable, and until then, nothing was worth time or energy. Those thoughts - that nobody else understood...flipped over and over, tumbling into each other and *becoming* each other, until the fear of knowing too much and the fear of knowing nothing stopped being different. The objective of the game was clear - Ultimate Mastery. If I couldn't prevent these horrors, I would destroy the unknown by imagining everything possible before it could happen.

This was not philosophical musing. It was a dark and disabling obsession.

I lived enraged that I been born into a world like this, and that I was expected to endure sudden tortures that I knew were ahead, but could *not* know when or how they would arrive.

Somewhere within those thoughts came the idea to imagine never having existed at all. Petrified of dying while wishing to 'not exist.' Everyone else cared about their *day*. They cared about friends and teacher and homework. I wanted to not die. Or if necessary, if the only way out of it was oblivion, then I wanted to have not existed in the first place. *"What do you want to be when you grow up?"* Well now…let us really look at my options.

And the fears of insanity started – as if the only place to hide (that wouldn't kill me) might be through a kind of self-implosion.

The truth behind the symbols:
Terror of the unknown springs from an archaic part of the mind. In a twist on an old saying, what we *think* are the objects of those fears may actually be *sheep* in wolf's costumes. Basic human insecurities may be dressed up as terrifying questions. Underneath those obsessions with death, infinity, the nature of reality and the meaning of human existence are realistic fears -- of rejection, abandonment, loss and loneliness. If unacknowledged, they take on mythic forms to frighten and fascinate us from a more detached vantage point. It is code written by our own minds with the purpose of fooling our own minds. We ruminate and suffer over symbols the mind invented as a way of avoiding earthly-bound questions.

Speaking of magical fantasies, today I wish I could go back in time and tell myself at the onset of those obsessions:

> *You are taking ordinary human fears and disguising them as unanswerable questions. Just like in a dream – what appears to be its content is only code in hyperbole. Anger at a friend produces a dream of the 2 of you in a dual to the death. Feeling unfairly criticized might generate dreams of violent and bloody attack. In states of disturbance, the unconscious (the dream weaver) <u>disguises ordinary fears as terrors of mythic proportion.</u>*

In waking states, obsessions with death and infinity and the nature of reality are standing in for very earthbound thoughts -- such as loneliness, rage or desire. You are not the devil you fear you are, nor the angel you think you must be. Unable (or unwilling) to accept your own humanity, you are taking ordinary feelings and disguising them as larger-than-life anxieties. Ordinary human needs.

There are *insider tips* that get learned the hard way during recovery. The suggestions in this chapter are not cures or magic bullets, but strategies from my own experience and those reported by other sufferers. They are effective ways to speed up recovery and more importantly, to avoid inadvertently making things worse.

Logic might dictate that someone would:
1) have a breakdown;
2) go to a professional.

Highly logical – but rare. Most of us are too afraid to admit what seems to be happening, and we try to recover without involving anyone else. With that in mind, this book positions *self*-help before professional help.

The morning after a hurricane is eerily quiet - a crisp wind, dark purple clouds, and a surreal cast to the sunlight. Neighbors poke through their yards, stepping over branches and broken chairs, nodding to acknowledge that everyone survived and this is the day for surveying damage.

Eventually, the worst symptoms will start to fade. One day you wake up - and something inside you is quieter. Not healed, not "normal" – and almost afraid to say so, but you finally feel a little bit better.

I think I'm actually okay…is it over? Am I going back to normal? Was it as bad as it seemed? How crippled am I? Can I repair completely?

Mental healing is not a steady climb. My first glimmers of improvement were followed by the worst anxiety I had ever felt. The slightest fear could escalate to terror within seconds, as if my emotional default was recalibrated for an overactive startle reflex.

Adding to the confusion, at times I actually felt *good* without explanation. I tried to believe that I was okay again, as if the mental storm had charged through my mind, wreaked some havoc and departed in the night.

It was a mistake to believe it was over. The symptoms had not suddenly vanished. It was more a state of remission that recovery. The entire experience was not likely to just undo itself, and by believing it could, I kept setting up intense disappointment.

I viewed the breakdown as something that happened *to* me – as if my brain had been struck by an unnamed illness. I wanted to heal, not change. I wanted everything to go back to the way it was before this nightmare – not realizing that would cause future ruptures.

HIDING FROM THE WORLD/ HIDING FROM THE SELF

A breakdown brings us face-to-face with ambivalence – which is a cruel bit of irony. Chances are, we once prided ourselves on our certainty – always knowing where we stood, exactly how we felt, precisely who we were, and why we wanted what we did. Seeing things in black and white with few conflicting thoughts, we probably forced round pegs into square holes to maintain a vision of a clear-cut world.

However, in reality humans are filled with ambivalence. We are a series of oppositional wishes, and the discovery of that truth is inevitable during a breakdown. It might also contribute to fears of insanity – bewildered by new emotions and thoughts, we interpret confusion as a precursor to madness. Certainty = sanity; the unknown = loss of self-control. Those conclusions are not true - not in the same realm - but they are common fantasies and fears.

- We want our symptoms to be seen and understood – AND - we desperately want to hide them from everybody around us;

- We have a strong desire to rip off social facades once and for all – AND - we make efforts every day to fasten those masks tighter than ever;

- *I'm sick! Why can't anyone see that?! AND -I need to keep telling myself I'm all right - pretending to be normal makes me feel better;*

- *Everybody expects too much of me and they don't understand what's going on inside my head...AND -Why do people look at me that way? I don't want to be treated like I'm crazy!*

Probably before the breakdown, we had similar conflicts (just not revolving around symptoms):

- *See* me – see the reality of who I am;

AND

- I am not what I appear to be; I can fool everyone and they will really touch me unless I choose to let them.

We spend extraordinary energy trying to deny ambivalent motives because we consider them highly dangerous. We still *have* them, of course – so even greater energy is invested in believing otherwise. *Knowing and not knowing*, we turn our free thoughts into dynamite. The dual awareness will create chronic anxiety – we live every minute with knowledge that one careless move could produce an explosion. Coming unraveled can be the result.

For some of us facades are nothing new. I spent years trying to be what other people wanted me to be (or what I thought they wanted). I developed good chameleon skills and in nearly every encounter, I responded more like an actor than participant. Being with people meant needing to figure out what they wanted and then convincing them I would provide it, or at least not oppose it. Being with people meant needing to control them – at the cost of turning myself inside out. And of course, being with anyone was utterly exhausting.

The masks also came with a perk. If I was rejected or criticized, it was only the façade being judged. The catch there is that only the façade was *liked* (or loved). And I resented that people were so blind to pretense – *why don't they look deeper? See who I am under here!* But if anyone looked too close, I lost interest.

All those unexpressed thoughts existed in a pressure cooker. And the more I smiled and submitted, the louder raged the thoughts that sought expression. Enter *ambivalence*.

Over time, the idea of exploding was both awful and appealing. Secretly held wishes that I might burst forth with every unexpressed word – not now, but one day…it could happen; of course it must never happen…but it could. And if so, it would be despite my best efforts. It would be a result of the masks wearing out. Therefore, not only would I be free, I would also be blameless.

That kind of fantasy sets the stage for anxiety attacks. It creates fears of losing control, or even of losing one's mind, because the harder the pretense, the tighter grows that pressure seal. Then when/if we want to *stop* pretending, the greater the fear of really losing control – which of course, makes pretense even more necessary. What began as a subtle way of controlling people becomes a compulsion designed to control a dangerous self. The drug felt so good at first, enhanced self-power…and was all within control. At first.

This theme will not apply to all anxiety attacks, but it is helpful to notice when the "façade versus authenticity" conflict rears its head. Ambivalent feelings will intensify after a breakdown. And if the fear of pending insanity is powerful, it could represent a battle between a fear of -- and simultaneous wish for – a chance to drop all masks.

LEARNING FROM EXPERIENCE
Teenagers and Recreational Drugs

Drug-Induced Symptoms

Sometimes teenagers come unraveled.
Teenagers often use recreational drugs.
Therefore, drugs damaged their brains.
Way too easy.

Naturally, it bears a valid warning: pot, mushrooms, ecstasy and acid are *Russian Roulette*. Some people use them and end up no worse for wear. But for anyone predisposed to anxiety, depressive or dissociative states, those drugs provide an instant trip to Hell. In addition, it is impossible to know if we *are* predisposed until the state has been induced, i.e., until it's too late.

Users may not have a bad experience during their altered state or even shortly thereafter. Symptoms can start weeks or months after the actual ingestion of a drug. The time-gulf between feeling the drug's effects (the "being high" experience) and the beginning of a breakdown is spent trying to re-establish the mind's status quo. Eventually, if those efforts fail, the mind perceives a massive assault to the entire mechanism. The drug experience caused a loss of status quo, and recovery attempts have failed. Self is unprotected. Breakdown.

While the use of drugs caused the rupture, it may have eventually happened *with or without drugs* – although not as fast or as furious. Perception-distorting chemicals put people face-to-face with thoughts they are unprepared to handle. The result can be loss of freedom within one's own mind.

Recreational? Think twice. Then think again. End of lecture.

However, *if you have **already done the drugs*** and now find yourself unraveling, remember: what you are currently experiencing is very similar to what other breakdown sufferers experience – *whether they ever used drugs or not.*

There are only so many ways the mind and imagination can go haywire, and the accounts of anxiety and depersonalization states reported by rec-drug users are the same as those of non-users. Anxiety is anxiety. Dissociation is dissociation. If a certain chemical caused permanent distortions, it would cause them consistently and nearly universally. That is not the case with most commonly used substances.

Don't add to your torment by blaming yourself for ruining your own mind. You did not break your brain. You broke down some defenses ruthlessly -- and way too suddenly -- inciting massive anxiety in response to a chemical crossing your blood/brain barrier. You may have enjoyed the trip, but part of your mind perceived it as trauma. *Too much was different too fast* - and ineffective defenses were called into action, trying to handle thoughts they were ill-equipped to even identify. The lingering trauma is likely that you no longer trust your own mind. Your brain itself has not been destroyed - the defenses that normally protect you have been shattered.

Just to clarify, some *perception distortions* seem to be physically based. They are usually the result of prolonged use of LSD, Mescaline or other hallucinogens. A syndrome called HPPD includes visual distortions of the optic receptors creating lingering images (" light trails") after abrupt movements, "seeing" vibrations and similar anomalies. There is however, a difference between true visual distortion (an hallucination, literally *seeing* trails of light when turning one's head) and the altered *awareness* of our own perceptions (*It's **as if** the room looks different; faces don't **seem to** look right, it **feels as if** my hands are too far away or too close or too large or too small*). Both disturbances can be very troubling, but there is a difference. In fact, the latter may be more frightening because it is so hard to describe. Everyone can imagine seeing trails of light (like after-images from a flashbulb), and consequently can empathize with those symptoms. But a vivid description of depersonalization invites wary looks from ordinary people – confirming our fears that we really are going insane.

In general, symptoms that inspire someone to buy this book will be the same symptoms experienced by *non*-drug users during a break-down. Severe anxiety and depersonalization states can feel as if they were pscyhotropically-induced because chemically-altering trips and dissociative experiences both invoke similar states of consciousness. One person's brain entered that state while tripping, and another opened the portal through dissociation or regression. However, the aspects of mind that *continue to produce symptoms* and *continue returning to those altered states of consciousness* are the same for both people.

If you recognize the thoughts and feelings described in this book, chances are good that you can recover with the kinds of help mentioned here.

But…after the hard climb back, hopefully you will not try said drugs again.

HIDING
Thoughts too strange to tell

We Are More Alike Than Different.

It is remarkable how unoriginal mental symptoms can be – people with unique histories describe nearly identical disturbing thoughts. Some ideas seem too frightening to ever tell – and those can be the most common.

Below are a few bizarre thoughts and illusions that often result from consistently disavowing strong emotions – especially anger. Obsessions can act as barriers between ourselves and the world – and more importantly, between ourselves and disturbing feelings. Everyone ruminates to a certain extent, and benefits from the distancing tactic.

Obsessions may take the form of delusional ideas – and those ideas themselves turn into our most terrifying secrets. *No sane person has thoughts like this. If anyone knew what really goes on inside my head, they would lock me up.* And those ideas reinforce the need to hide even more.

Unspeakable Thoughts that might sound familiar:

- I am dead. My death already happened, but I refuse to believe it. This nervous breakdown was my brain's way of shutting down – to avoid having to see that I'm dead, that I'm nothing but a ghost hovering in a netherworld between former reality and an eternal abyss.

- I am insane, and my thoughts are delusions. I could be locked in a secure hospital room and imagining or only dreaming this existence. The world in *front* of me is the delusion, not the ideas inside my head.

- I am having premonitions. The terrible anxiety and panic is a warning of something horrible just ahead – something no one else knows yet. There is a Reason for these terrors – I know or can see something is coming. In isolation, I'm foreseeing my own death.

- I am gaining secret enlightenment. There are truths about life that I see too clearly, as if it is more than I can handle. This breakdown brought insights – and rather than being signs of illness, my distorted feelings are an awakening. Fearing I'm not strong enough to deal with the awareness, I feel excited and terrified that I may have a special destiny.

The hidden thoughts we believe no one else could comprehend are held by many people in the throes of nervous illness – equally afraid to say them out loud. We may be the most alike when feeling completely alone.

Find someone you trust and talk about your darker thoughts. Letting the unspeakable ideas find audible words can detonate the most destructive aspect – the power they hold over you *because* they are secrets.

3 Things You <u>Don't</u> Want To Do

Actually, that is a misleading title. You *will* want to do these things -- every one of them. You are probably compelled to do them daily. Nonetheless, try as hard as possible to:

- …RESIST taking your emotional temperature.
    We all know this one. It has become our primary activity during every waking moment.
    How anxious do I feel this morning?
    Is the trembling still bad? Is my hand steadier than it was this afternoon? Is the left hand shakier than the right?
    Am I still feeling that disorientation? I'm not dizzy, but there is something odd, like a feeling of drifting…
    Do I feel worse after walking outside? My mood feels more hopeless than yesterday; am I starting a downward spiral?
    Do I feel more connected, more real than before I went to bed?
    Or do I feel strange right now because I'm thinking about it? Maybe I was calmer a minute ago before I had this thought… (Feel free to add your personal favorites, try to laugh about it, then try your hardest to stop these patterns).

- …RESIST the urge to read everything you can find about severe mental & physical illness (this is the *Curse of the Internet* – I was ill long before information was at our fingertips, so at least I had to venture out to a library in order to terrify myself).

- ….RESIST acting on self-dares done in the name of **mastery**….(not the empowering kind of mastery, but false bravado)

    > Be suspect of the any effort that leads you right back to the edge of your fears again and again. It is an easy trap because we fool ourselves into believing it must be courageous and in our self-interest. In truth, we are sabotaging the progress like Penelope unweaving her loom.

    As soon as I felt more grounded, I ventured back to the realm of disturbing thoughts. It seemed I could demystify the terrors by making myself face them, *study* them…in short, ***obsess about them***. It was the same old pattern with a new twist.

    I tricked myself by reasoning *"well, that's what therapy does – examines the cause, shines light on our fears."* But therapy is very different from what I was doing to myself – and even at the time I realized it. Re-engaging our demons does not feel like discovery or growth. It is only false bravado – we whistle our way through the graveyard (while secretly shaking).

And I know - it can be highly seductive.

Resist creeping back to the ledge. There are other ways to examine causes without turning them into new obsessions and sources of daily fear. If you are scaring yourself on purpose, it will be clear. Now as you read those words, do *not* start down the tunnel of worrying about why you would want to scare yourself in the first place. That is only more of same.

The point is: Don't work hard by day to weave yourself together only to pull it all apart, thread by thread in the darkness.

Those three mind games slow down the process of healing more than you could ever imagine.

They are counterproductive to every effort at strengthening your confidence and sense of self. They are more than wasted energy – they are self-harm.

PLEASE TELL ME WHAT TO DO!

"I'll do <u>anything</u> to feel right again!"

Well, sure, you say that *now*…

Some people cannot fully recover from long-standing emotional or nervous illness because recovery is made or broken by what we do **when we feel** ***better*** – not while still lost in the abyss.

In the darkest hour, of course we make deals with God, and promise anything to regain our mind. *"Change? No problem. You won't even recognize the Old Me…"* But gradually start feeling *stronger*, and watch yourself go back to the most familiar ways of thinking. It's almost a return to the scene of the crime – as if trying to prove that you're better now, tougher now, safe enough that nothing really needs to change after all.

And you might pull it off. But more likely, you will feel okay for awhile, re-set the same patterns that got you into the original mess, keep denying the reality of cause & effect, and unwittingly wait for the *next* breakdown.

The work gets done when we're stronger. Unfortunately, that may not be when we feel desperate enough to try.

One of the games I used to play with myself was this:
All I wanted was to get better.
I was willing to do whatever it took.
I was more than willing to let a trusted professional fix me – and even get the credit!
But at the end of the day, the one thing I did *not* want to do was change.

For Long-Term Sufferers

There is absolutely no average time for recovery. Each of us is unique, and we have histories that are complicated and individual. Some will find a fast path out, and look back on their bizarre experience with wonder.

Early treatment is clearly a good idea. That is not to imply if left untreated, your symptoms will degenerate into a worse condition. The danger is that over long periods of time, we continue to reinforce bad reactions to learned fears. We form patterns that develop into habits, and the more entrenched we become in *bad* habits, the harder we will find it to change. However, the duration of any nervous illness may have as much to do with genetics as with learned response. Again, no easy answers and no guarantees.

I was far from being a *quick fix*. My symptoms lasted years – *many years* – and they went from bad to worse --to slightly better - to worse than ever. It is never too early to work on yourself - and it is never too late. After many efforts at treatment, different medications and many different doctors, I reached a point of resignation. I 'knew' I was permanently ill and that the most I could hope for was just something to keep me from getting worse. I was wrong. The day I found the therapy and doctor who would turn out to be my key to recovery, I was looking only for refills on a med. I believed there was nothing I had not tried, and felt destined to grow old deeply entrenched in illness.

No matter how long (or how briefly) you have been ill – there is hope. Keep searching for a form of treatment that resonates with your particular personality, and keep fighting the temptation to slink into more self-obsession. There is no magic cure and no universal solution. But time itself does not indicate hopelessness. Keep fighting for your own mental freedom. The optimism of this book does *not* reflect my personality during the years of illness. I was utterly without hope, furious that symptoms had destroyed my life, and terrified that the nightmare might only grow worse. I worked towards recovery while filled with pessimism and fear.

It is never too late. And a positive attitude is not required. Keep searching.

SUGGESTIONS

Below is a summary of suggestions that appear throughout this book, followed by a chart of key points.

These things really help -- regardless of the type of symptom, or how long you have been ill. Give them serious attention and your recovery will be both faster and steadier.

1) **Outward actions**
With a case of the flu, it feels right to spend the day in bed, drifting in and out of sleep, as if solitude and silence are conducive to healing. It may work for the flu, but isolation is a bad idea during a breakdown.

Stay involved in the ordinary day-to-day world. Resist the temptation to put everything on hold until you heal. You may justify the self-care by calling it a "much needed rest." That sounds great, but having been there, I know you are *not* resting. Instead, you are *obsessing* about every thought and feeling, terrifying yourself minute-by-minute over sensations that cannot be described. Keep it up long enough and an implosion can result – already detached from the real world, it begins to feel like you are tumbling backwards into timeless self-awareness. Alice falling down the rabbit hole, and still falling and falling longer...until your mind becomes a place that seems to exist beyond time and distance. **And it will take much more effort to climb back *up* than it took you to tumble down.**

Distinguish between taking care of yourself and sheltering yourself. Spending weeks in quiet darkness will set you up to feel over-stimulated by ordinary activities. When that flu patient finally gets out of bed, the world will initially seem very fast and loud and disturbingly bright. Those perceptions are magnified even more in emotional illness. Keep moving. Don't let every-day-life get too far away.

2) **Making peace with bad advice**
"Just don't *think* about everything so much." At some point, a well-meaning friend or family member will say that and ignite your anger. Try to remember how little you knew about mental symptoms before this

breakdown. It would be great if people could understand – but do not expect it. The only thing you have any control over is your own response.

Nodding and mumbling *"that could be true, you could be right"* may be the most intelligent choice. Trying to explain why their suggestion is absurd takes the energy you need to conserve for recovery itself. Plus – *they still will not get it.* Find other sufferers and/or mental health professionals and share the details of your symptoms. As far as family and friends are concerned, accept that they are very worried – and that they feel powerless to do anything constructive. Look for the compassion behind their misguided efforts, and let it go at that – not for them, but for your own sake.

3) **Inner monologue**

Human beings cannot *not* think. We have running inner monologues throughout the day. We "talk" to ourselves about feelings, plans, things we wish we had said, things we want to say, decisions, actions, revised decisions, memories good and bad. But right after a breakdown, we tend to expunge any thought not related to illness.

Encourage the kinds of thoughts you *would* be having if the breakdown had never happened. In much the same way we know how to go through the motions of looking like a "normal" person, try to *think* the *thoughts* of the more normal version of you. Yes, it's phony and forced, but remember - the more tempting option of obsessing over your mental state is not authentic either. Better to choose the more productive pretense than surrender to compulsions generated by your symptom. You cannot hyper-focus on every sensation while consciously trying to run an interior monologue revolving around ordinary life. At first, it seems impossible to not self-watch, but you can choose *how* you do the watching. Silently describe to yourself what you see, hear, and taste rather than what you fear, feel, or imagine. Describe what you notice "out there" in reality, rather than anything you notice inside your own head. Resist constantly giving words (especially silent ones) to the sensations that scare you. Stay with the tangible, the pragmatic and the sensory.

And encourage observations about same to fill your silent thoughts.

4) **Common sense**
We all know this stuff: proper diet, moderate exercise, consistent sleep habits, reduce or eliminate alcohol, drugs and caffeine.

If recovering patients actually *did* those things, they would significantly speed up their own healing. I failed miserably, insisting that food intake and sleep habits had nothing whatsoever to do with how I felt. *"This is not about balanced meals! My brain is collapsing!"* I did notice that caffeine was an awful idea even in small amounts. And I often slept way too much, not too little. Sleep was a place to hide, a way station of non-thought. But excessive sleep can be as disorienting as a lack of it.

The things we know to do (and always knew to do) are the hardest to actually make ourselves **do**.
Remember to use what you already know.

5) **Structured routine**
Breakdown symptoms are all-consuming. It is easy to become lost in a daily world of half-waking/half-dreams. An hour, a day and a week have meaning only according to fears that mount and recede, moods that worsen and fade. Your brain and nervous system become your new clock and calendar, and the universe itself seems to matter only according to the strange sensations within your mind. Dangerous territory. It is crucial to stay connected to time and place - set patterns for every day – go to bed and get up at certain hours, take planned walks, make dates, develop a schedule. Eat three meals (or whatever works for you) consistently. Keep a routine. Naturally, you will deviate from time to time, but you will realize it is deviation. Chronic listlessness will keep you in a twilight state (*"is it morning or night?"*). Daily life cannot be set in stone, but you need to set it in *something*.

6) **Connections to people**

One of the most grounding things a human being can do is to talk with another person – the back and forth exchanging of ideas, listening and linking and responding, being stimulated by someone else's thoughts and watching your own have an impact in return. *Stay in contact with others.*

7) **Remember Reality**
At every opportunity remind yourself that magical thinking, good-luck rituals and obsessive mental games are dangerous. They might offer comfort, but it is only temporary – and every single time you allow yourself to play along with *"well, just in case there is such a thing as magic, it can't really hurt..."* you are keeping yourself ill.   At every turn, choose the logical linear approach to fears and worries.

Suggestions Chart

What helps:	*Remember:*
Outward actions	*Do* something. Every minute spent ruminating, questioning, worrying & experimenting with your own mind is a step backwards. You can return to philosophical exercises once you're better. For now, keep *doing* life, not pondering it.
Make peace with bad advice	The only person you have any control over is you. Overall, your family and friends will not understand what's happening with you. That does not mean you are unreachable – or beyond comprehension. It only means that most people have tremendous difficulty & fear around the subject of mental suffering. And there is very little you can do or say to change that.
Inner monologue	Keep sensory inner commentary going. Describe to yourself what you see, hear, touch, smell. Keep the silent inner talk about practical, tangible realities. Don't feed life's unanswerable questions.
Common Sense	Use everything you already know that works – good diet, sleep habits, exercise, etc. You have an arsenal of helpful information -- use it.
Structured routine	Create a daily routine. Stick to it, or change it, but avoid listless drifting that ignores time and space. When you sleep, set an alarm. Make plans that will happen at specific times. You may or may not keep them – but make them. Keep structure in your daily life.
Connections to people	Talk. Listen. And talk some more. Even if nobody seems to understand, keep connecting through words. Nothing is more grounding. At times, you will say it makes no difference. You will believe you might as well just stay alone. At those times, reach out even harder.
Keep choosing reality	Resist the lure of magical thoughts, compulsions and rituals. It is almost impossible to fully recover while trying to serve both reality and magic.

Understanding Treatment Options –
What exactly are we trying to treat?

Defining the Problem:
The human mind is constantly assessing and responding to danger. One response to perceived threats is *signal anxiety* – the Central Nervous System's "fight or flight" instinct sends extra adrenaline into a body that must make a snap decision – either start running for safety or prepare a counter attack. At least, those would be options in a predator-filled jungle. In our more ordinary lives, we become all hyped-up and left with no one to fight and no place to run.

Important: perceived danger can incite many symptoms other than anxiety and panic. It can also be the root cause of severe depression, obsessions, compulsions, and dissociation – all states of mind that seem unrelated to anxiety or adrenaline. But as a response to signal anxiety, the brain may reject both fight and flight, redirecting the unused aggression into *itself* (a common cause of depression). Again, our genetics probably determine what reaction gets "chosen" and subsequently which symptoms appear.

Phobias usually organize around *external* threats – fear of heights, water, animals, fire, violent assault, etc. Likewise, anxiety attacks can be provoked by dread of something "out there." But dangers are both external and internal – externally, jeopardy of our bodily well-being; internally, jeopardy to our sense of who we are. *Internal* dangers signal threats to the cohesion of self - with identity at stake rather than limbs.

In response to those threats, we act to preserve the consistency with which we see ourselves (integrity of self). Self-image is a measure of status quo – and is comprised of ideals, roles, values that we adopt during a lifetime. That status quo becomes a filter through which we pass every potential thought and impulse. Thoughts are *unacceptable* when they do not fit into the peg holes that define our identity.

I am safe. I know precisely who I am.
To guard such beliefs, the mind will distort reality, deny its own thoughts and continually monitor itself to keep irreconcilable ideas far apart. *I am consistent, un-hypocritical, solid. I may tell a lie sometimes,*

but I know I'm lying. When it comes to the fundamentals of myself, I encounter no surprises.

Any potential new thought gets the green light only if compatible with the rules I use for defining "I."
I am this way; I am not like that at all.
Here is something I would never think and never want – while this is something I am committed to forever.

Threats to our cherished self-perceptions are as significant as life-and-death. If self-cohesion is under attack, a symbolic form of death is possible and the mind will instantly employ massive defenses to prevent it.

A breakdown is the "breaking down" of that feeling of safety. Our methods of assessing and avoiding danger failed us, or at least we believe they did.

Those 2 common terrors – death and madness - symbolize the 2 ultimate disasters of unheeded danger.
Externally = death.
Internally = insanity.

A breakdown leads to a scary conclusion: *whatever I had been doing to assess danger has stopped working. I am no longer safe in the world – not from what may be **out there**, and not from the contents of my own mind.* And that thought makes us freeze like a wild animal in headlights.

Important: Your reactions to danger will not be permanently distorted. Imagine a traumatized burglary victim installing an elaborate security system after being robbed. For awhile, your mind will be over-reactive because the nervous system is setting *extra* alarms. Those new hair-trigger responders are functioning as a kind of alarm's alarm – detecting anything remotely likely to trip the regular system. We feel hyper-reactive because we *are* hyper-reactive - the body is functioning post-trauma. It is temporary.

The Basics of Treatment

To simplify options, keep in mind that every conventional treatment boils down to one of two approaches (or a combination). Symptoms of a breakdown will be treated by:

Approach #1: Exploring **what activated** our inner alarms; or

Approach #2: Exploring ways to **modify the alarm system** so it won't trip as easily.

Approach 1 –
Targeting our Thinking
- assumes the nervous system/brain activity is performing correctly and that the breakdown was the result of perceived dangers bypassing the mind's usually reliable defenses and causing a rupture. The question becomes: what was perceived as so threatening and what can be done to develop less traumatic reactions to future threats?

Treatments include:

- Psychodynamic therapies - patients examine their thoughts, beliefs, memories in search of greater self-understanding;
- Cognitive therapies – searching for the core beliefs and conscious thoughts that trigger symptom responses;
- Behavioral therapy – works towards desensitization of perceived danger through incremental exposure to feared action or idea.

Approach 2 –
Targeting our Neurochemistry
- assumes the brain's neurotransmissions are *not* responding properly (over-activated, under-reactive, etc.) The question becomes: what malfunctioned inside the brain, and how to correct it?

Treatments include:
- Medications

This is where most people start -- with the plea *"make this horrible feeling go away!"* Medication is a logical choice. If it works, it will be fairly quick. If it works, it may be a good adjunct to other treatment options down the line. But bear in mind, it may *not* work.

During the medication discussion, your doctor will probably suggest drugs that target anxiety and/or depression – based on the belief that most symptoms (mentioned in this book) persist because of an underlying **depressive** or **anxiety** state. Treat the main symptom, and the mind should re-stabilize. Lowering the patient's anxiety level will reduce all of their anxiety-based symptoms. Lift a patient's mood and depression-based symptoms should decrease. This does not always work, but it has a decent track record and the response is fairly quick.

I reached the point of wanting to scream "Every single symptom can't be anxiety or depression!" Actually, they almost can. Those two categories have become so broad that they are included in most psychiatric diagnoses.

There are pragmatic reasons for bringing Anxiety and Depression into the picture.
- Both are usually responsive to medication.
- Both are accepted by most insurance companies as treatable disorders.

Whether or not you officially *have* one, it is worth determining if your symptoms are anxiety and/or depression-*based*. They are the salt and pepper of most psychiatric diagnoses.

If medication works, talk with the doctor about a projected length of time to continue it. The answers will probably be:
short-term for anti-anxiety meds;
longer term for anti-depressants.

Those are generalities based on the properties of the drugs, not an implication that depression is harder to treat.

A successful stint on medication may be enough to eliminate symptoms. Or it may not.
With temporary chemical help, a patient's neurochemistry may stabilize and be able to maintain its normal state without continued meds. Sufficiently calmed, the brain stops defaulting to anxiety as a ground of being, or once depression has lifted, the mind may regain the ability to sustain a balanced mood.

In those cases, treatment succeeded by inhibiting strong emotion(s) long enough to allow the brain to resume its former functions. It does not address what caused the disruption in the first place. In other words, whatever put the mind under siege is still lurking. The brain is just no longer firing back.

Pharmacological Treatment
also called
Medication Maintenance
– the patient is being treated *exclusively* with medication. Likely includes:
- a consultation or two,
- follow-up contact to determine how successfully a new treatment is or isn't working,
- (approximate) monthly visits for continued assessment and maintaining of prescriptions.

Keep in mind - this is not therapy. However, the psychiatrist may also have a private therapy practice and treat patients short or long-term.

Any doctor you see for Medication Maintenance should tell you:
- *why a particular drug is being suggested for you;*
- *the reasoning behind the overall treatment plan;*
- *specifically what the pills are believed to do;*
- *what to expect in terms of side effects & primary effects.*

If considering medication - choose a psychiatrist.

Technically, your family doctor (or any M.D.) can give psychiatric meds -- but that only gets you a prescription. You need more – you need sound advice, reassurance and assessment. For an evaluation of emotional/mental symptoms, it is essential to see someone in the mental health field.

Do not avoid "the psychiatrist route" because it sounds ominous. *Maybe I don't have anything serious if I only see my regular doctor.* Big mistake. True, you may not have a serious problem, but only someone with appropriate education and professional experience can assess nervous/emotional symptoms. This is your brain at stake – use good sense.

Seeking Help
-- Talking With A Professional --

Patient – *I know I have a hiatal hernia.*
        Doctor – *What makes you think so?*
Patient – *Because my stomach hurts.*

If you tell a psychiatrist that you self-diagnosed from a book or the Internet, that is pretty much how you will sound. Mental health professionals realize it is easy for us to recognize ourselves in descriptions of symptoms because the anxiety over *not* knowing has inspired a quick answer. A psychiatrist may assume that whatever you think you "have" is just the most recent disorder you found in print.

It is more beneficial to suggest what you think applies to you. Rather than insisting on what you've *got*, tell how you feel -- and how often you feel that way. Describe the sensations and thoughts that prevent you from functioning -- and how often your life is handicapped by them.

And... tell all of it. That will be hard – because we all have dark and odd ideas. Deep down, we are so afraid of sounding "crazy," we imagine being locked away if we disclose our truly bizarre thoughts. Just be as forthcoming as possible, and remember:
- doctors know what to listen for; and
- psychiatrists have already heard it all.

Also, watch for a tendency to hide behind **Patient Code** (we all do this at first). We assume, or at least hope, that a doctor can somehow read between the lines and hear what we really mean behind casual words.

Patient Says: (hoping to be understood)	**Patient Really Means:** (but is too afraid to say)
I feel anxious.	*I'm positive I'm going insane.*
I can't seem to relax.	*If I let go for an instant, I'll plummet into a terror so overpowering I'll never come out of it.*
I just don't feel like myself.	*I feel like I no longer exist or that I'm living in a terrifying dream.*
I'm not motivated; can't seem to get moving....	*If left alone, I would spend every day, without exception, lying in bed.*
How can we be sure it won't get worse?	*I have <u>horrible</u> thoughts. Are you 100 per cent positive I won't leap off a building or go berserk and stab myself?*
So you believe its just anxiety?	*What specific signs can I watch for to know if I'm schizophrenic?*
It's getting harder to hold myself together.	*My mind is clenched like a fist, but if I let my thoughts run free, the results would be catastrophic.*

Too fragile for therapy?

During my worst symptoms, I lacked the strength to do anything in therapy except show up. Sometimes we need to be helped out of crisis first, and a good professional will recognize precarious states. Treatment can be approached with those needs in mind. Don't fall into the trap of believing you need to feel better before seeking help.

Therapy may not be for everyone. But if it is something you want to explore, there is no need to wait till you feel stronger.

Simply *talking* with a mental health professional can provide:

- Reassurances and information about what's happening to you (and what's *not* happening).

- A way to keep emotions flowing. While a broken bone heals, many otherwise *healthy* muscles atrophy from lack of movement. During a breakdown, we can similarly freeze our emotions – scared to feel, scared to express. But trying to live in stasis is counterproductive to healing. Talking encourages spontaneous thoughts and feelings, and can prevent you from trying to put yourself on hold.

- A chance to explore some of your thoughts just prior to the breakdown.

- Guidance on what you can do during the worst of the feelings, and pitfalls to avoid.

MEDICATION
Whether or not to try medication is an individual decision and one that should be made only after discussions with a trusted doctor.

Psychiatric medication is certainly a loaded subject. If you broach it with family or friends, be prepared for very strong opinions (pro and con). The reality, of course, is somewhere in the middle.

A Few Subjective Truths about Psychiatric Medication

- It will not destroy your brain nor will it make everything okay.
- It might help you to feel and function better. And it might not.
- It will come with some side effects.
- No one knows exactly how or why psychiatric medications work.
- People say it helped them tremendously – some swearing it literally saved their lives.
- People say psychiatric meds made their symptoms worse (or caused new and more disturbing ones).
- It is reported that psychiatric drugs allow some people to be fully functional for the first time in their lives.
- It is reported that psychiatric medications can produce serious withdrawal reactions that may linger for years after the drug has been stopped.

My Personal Experience and opinions:
Over a period of years, I tried many different medications, most of which barely helped, and a couple that were useful in reducing symptoms.
I have no horror stories from taking any of them, but I also had limited success. And I have heard a few first-hand accounts from patients who experienced very bad reactions. One thing I know -- each person's experience will be different.

Meds may be able to jump-start a feeling of safety, or lift a mood out of deep depression. But no med can keep us in those states if we counteract their effects (knowingly or not). Unless therapy is used in conjunction with pills, success is often short-lived. It makes little sense to swallow chemicals in hopes of feeling better while continuing to think and behave in the same ways that created the symptoms in the first place. That is asking too much of any pill -- even those yet to be invented.

Universal Truths about Medication

- It is a terrible idea to try anyone else's psychiatric drug - ever. Depending on underlying symptoms and dormant conditions, what soothes one person can provoke traumatic reactions in someone else.

- Always take meds exactly as directed – if you disagree with your doctor's instructions, say so. Discuss it, debate it, and remind the expert that ultimately you are the authority on your own body's response. However, doing things your own way without informing the doctor is a mistake.

- Likewise, report if you take any other drugs (legal or illegal). Honest communication is vital when using medicine that crosses the blood/brain barrier – as psychiatric meds do.

- Report every single side-effect. Assume full responsibility for describing what seems to be happening within your body. *"Well, the doctor should have known..."* will only be slightly comforting when you are debilitated.

SEEKING HELP
Who's Who in Mental Health?

If considering medication or therapy, you may encounter these professional titles:
- **Psychiatrist**
- **Psychologist**
- **Psychoanalyst**
- **Social worker**
- **Nurse practitioner**
- **Therapist**
- **Counselor**

It is a good idea to know who does *what* (and their training and background) before deciding on someone to meet.

Three factors to consider while shopping for a therapist:

    I.   **Education and professional credentials.**

    II.   **Patient/therapist fit**

    III.   **The type of therapy that person practices**

I. Education and Professional Credentials

Psychiatrist: a Medical Doctor specializing in mental and emotional illness. The title guarantees they have:
- graduated Medical School,
- completed a residency term at a hospital (under doctors' supervision),
- can prescribe medications.

A psychiatrist completed a hospital residency (working with chronically ill patients, including people in psychotic states). Granted, if suffering a nervous breakdown, you are way at the *other* end of that scale -- but experience in treating the seriously ill can improve empathy and communication skills for work with patients along the entire spectrum.

A *"Board Certified"* psychiatrist is even better. That title is evidence the doctor has met standards & successfully passed testing by a Psychiatric Board of the American Medical Association. Aside from proving academic strength, it shows ongoing commitment to their field.

Who's Who In Mental Health (continued)

Clinical Psychologist:
– another well-respected title. Should hold at least a Master's degree. If also a Ph.D., there will be a *"Dr."* before the therapist's name (standing for *"doctor of philosophy"* in the study of psychology). This indicates thorough training, but remember this kind of *"Dr."* is not a m*edical* doctor and therefore, cannot prescribe medication. A well-trained clinical psychologist may have had more academic exposure to theories of mind and abnormal psychology than psychiatrists (who tend to get most of their experience with patients during residency – and often *learn* therapy while *conducting* their first therapies).

Psychoanalyst:
– Someone trained to conduct personal psychoanalysis. May also offer psychotherapy. May or may not be a medical doctor. May or may not be a "therapist" in addition to being an analyst.
– There are no educational pre-requisites to study analysis. Medical doctors, psychologists, psychotherapists (among other professionals) can enter a training program to become analysts. As a consumer, the important question is this: from *which institute* did they receive the analytic training? There are highly reputable ones that require candidates to undergo personal analysis themselves, and supervise their early treatment cases. Excellent training and experience. But *investigate* - anyone can call themselves an analyst. Ask about their training institute, affiliations, certification and degrees.

Social worker:
– sometimes called an "MSW" indicating a *Masters Degree* in Social Work. If holding a Master's, their education probably included clinical psych experience, working under supervision while seeing patients in a therapy setting.

– If only an undergraduate degree, they may have no formal psych training. Rather than therapy, the interactions are probably of a "counseling" nature. This professional may also hold certificates of training in crisis work, addiction counseling, etc. Ask.

Who's Who In Mental Health (continued)

Nurse Practitioner:
- holds an advanced nursing degree and probably works closely with a specific team of doctors or a single M.D. A Nurse Practitioner can prescribe medication – as part of an on-going treatment plan once the patient consults with a psychiatrist. The N.P. will monitor the medication maintenance – assessing dosage, responsiveness to different meds, refilling prescriptions, etc. This professional will not engage in on-going therapy with patients, but serves primarily in a support position. If the N.P. is also a hospital staff psychiatric nurse, the experience level could be quite high. Usually very knowledgeable, can provide useful and accurate answers to your questions.

Counselor:
– Ask, ask ask….about training and background. The title of *counselor* does not denote any specific training or experience. Also, take into account that a counselor is probably affiliated with a specific institution (a school, a church, etc). The slant of the counseling will be determined by that framework, which is not inherently good or bad – just another factor to consider.

Caution: Like *counselor*, the title of *therapist* has no legitimate meaning (except implying "someone who practices therapy"). Anyone can call themselves a therapist. Look for the credentials behind that title.

II. "Fit" between therapist and patient

Ultimately this can be more important than any impressive background or degree. The good news is there is nothing complex about looking for fit. We know it when we see it. The bad news is that is can be tough to find. *Fit* includes the qualities we value when meeting anyone new – especially someone likely to play an important role in our lives.

Do you like being with this person? Look for personal chemistry between you – an ability to connect – through words and empathic expressions.

Ideally, you feel *heard*. That is not the same as feeling understood - which might not be possible, especially at first. But the therapist should be listening attentively in an effort to understand.

You should feel a desire to listen back – not feeling intimidated, but able to recognize that the therapist has some expertise. By the end of the consultation phase, if the fit is right, you will know.

This does not mean that every session will be harmonious. If you choose a long-term depth therapy, conflict is part of the process, and there will be times you despise the professional who is trying to help. All the more reason to choose someone you like at the beginning – that authentic connection comes in handy during rougher hours.

Also, consider qualities that matter to **you**. Some people would be annoyed by a witty therapist. Personally, I need one with a great sense of humor (of course "great" is defined as similar to my own). You are entitled to work with someone you *like*. Search for it.

	Can *prescribe meds*	*Title* **guarantees**:	***Should*** *have:*	***Services*** *probably offered:*
Psychiatrist	Yes	Graduated Medical school and a hospital residency term under supervision.	Board Certification	Medication Maintenance Psychotherapy Consultation/ Assessment
Psychologist		Psychology degree	Ph. D *or* Master's degree	Psychotherapy (psychodynamic, CBT, Depth, eclectic, etc.).
Psychoanalyst	*		Affiliation with a reputable psychoanalytic Institute; An advanced academic degree (possibly M.D.)	Psycho-analysis Depth-based psychotherapy
MSW/Social Worker		Sociology Degree MSW = Master's in Social Work	Clinical counseling experience under supervision	Psychotherapy Supportive Therapy and/or counseling
Counselor			Strong affiliation with reputable organization	Supportive Counseling
Nurse Practitioner	Yes	Master's in Nursing	Strong working relationship with clinical psychiatrist or psychiatric facility	Medication maintenance (in conjunction w/ psychiatrist) supportive counseling

- Maybe (if also a Medical Doctor).

*"Sit in this room and say **what**? It's beyond language. You don't get it, I'm sorry, there aren't words for what's happening to me..."*

"Then we'll find words," he said. And treatment began.

Therapy

Unraveling
What Got Us Here

III. What kind of therapy?

In addition to a professional title, you need to consider the *type* of treatment a therapist practices. Psychiatrists and psychologists choose to work with a form of therapy that reflects their beliefs about the mind and the meaning of symptoms. **Those beliefs differ widely from theory to theory.**

Do not assume that entering treatment will give you access to a pool of collective psychiatric knowledge. There are precious little irrefutable facts about emotional illness and symptoms. As therapy patients we are purchasing *specific* knowledge and ideas belonging to one school of thought. Treatment techniques, breakthroughs, etc. are shared within those circles, among professionals who already share a fundamental theory about the mind. Therapists will not be privy to the latest ideas in a radically different school of thought (nor would they be interested in those, anyway).

With that in mind, the **kind of therapy** you choose determines the information and techniques that will be available to you during the entire course of your treatment. It is well worth investigating to find one that resonates with your views on the human mind.

One starting point is to imagine the popular therapies along a continuum. At one end are the behavioral therapies, and at the other end is psychoanalysis - with most treatment approaches falling along the middle. This continuum is based on the following:

    1)   **Therapies that target symptoms *directly*** – patients learn techniques to curb the thoughts and behaviors that exacerbate anxiety, depression, obsessions, etc.;

    Short-term behavioral therapies:

- 1-2 sessions per week or less;
- Short-term commitment (several sessions to several months);
- Treatment is focused on symptoms only. Includes practical suggestions, relaxation techniques, tools for modifying behavior in efforts to break the patterns that perpetuate symptoms.

2) **Therapies that target symptoms** *indirectly* – patients examine the feelings, thoughts and conflicts that provoked the breakdown, using self-knowledge to heal the disturbances that symptoms represent.

Psychoanalysis:
- Sessions of 4+ times per week;
- Long-term commitment (think years, not months);
- Treatment delves deep – working with the unconscious, anxiety may *increase* temporarily.
- Huge potential for growth/change. The focus is on character that was formed early and is serving as structure to the adult self/personality. Treatment addresses the entire person, rather than full focus on symptoms.

In a gross over-simplification, any therapy that is closer to Example 1 will be shorter (with a potentially faster reduction in some symptoms), but not effective at reaching the source of the problem. Consequently, the results are often less dramatic and the patient is less protected against relapses down the line. Therapies closer to Example 2 require a longer time investment, but offer the potential for significant and permanent change.

At various places along that spectrum are other popular treatments: psychodynamic therapy, cognitive, cognitive-behavioral ("CBT"), analytic-based psychotherapy, eclectic, Rational-Emotive, etc.

This explains why one person's experience of treatment can be radically different from someone else's. There is no such thing as "regular talk therapy." Consider the following different interpretations of an Anxiety Attack:

A Psychoanalyst views powerful anxiety as the result of disturbing or opposing thoughts. The symptom is considered a *symbol* for disturbances in the field, rather than a sign of illness. Treatment involves identifying conflicts and putting words to the unacknowledged thoughts provoking the symptom-reaction.

A Behavioral therapist, defining anxiety within the bio-chemical position, sees a panic attack as a misdirection of the body's response to "fight or flight" instinct, and encourages the patient to master activities that have been phobically avoided.

A Cognitive therapist might describe anxiety attacks as the patient's learned response to stimulation, and work towards redirecting thoughts to create different responses and modulate degrees of reaction.

The foundation of a therapist's approach is not negotiable. Choose a treatment based on ideas you fundamentally agree with, or you may doom the process before it starts. It is a guaranteed waste of time (and money) to expect a behavioral therapist to examine the unconscious or childhood memories. Likewise, a patient will not be able to elicit daily coping techniques from an analyst.

The following is a quick tour of the marketplace. These are popular mainstream treatments that I am familiar with, and exclusions only reflect my lack of personal knowledge. Any of these can be helpful for treating symptoms described in this book.

Is one type of therapy more effective at curing symptoms?
No. If there was, you would have heard about it. Its proponents would be advertising from the rooftops "here is a technique finally *proven* to work!"

Every type of therapy treatment has success stories and failures. The best summation of why/how any of them work may be: *ultimately what heals is the relationship between patient and therapist, engaged in mutual dedicated effort to find something the patient can do to reduce his/her own distress.* Most successfully treated patients (regardless of the type of therapy) would probably agree.

UnconventionalAlternative Treatments: For the reader who is looking for a non-traditional therapy, my only advice is: listen to your gut.
I believe most non-mainstream treatments are harmless (although very

questionable in terms of actual results). But common sense will announce loud and clear if you encounter something completely off the wall – and they are definitely out there -- either *"too good to be true,"* or *"too bizarre to be possible,"* or *"too preachy to be helpful"*. Even though you are frightened and confused, use your common sense. No one should push you to experiment with any form of treatment that doesn't feel right.

TREATMENT OPTIONS
Cognitive/Behavioral Therapies

Behavioral Therapy –
This treatment focuses exclusively on the Now. Patients learn to redirect their current actions– and ultimately to re-train automatic behaviors into new patterns that prove satisfying instead of distressing. Techniques include positive/negative reinforcements aimed at unlearning habits that are consistently invoked by certain stimuli.

Cycle/vicious circle of thoughts generating emotions generating more worried thoughts.

There is very little, if any, focus on *how* the patients got this way (beyond needing to identify troublesome patterns). Attention goes into changing *present problems* that are being caused by *present behaviors*. Phobias may be effectively treated using Behavioral Therapy.

Cognitive-Behavioral Therapy – (often called CBT)
Uses the basic techniques of the behavioral therapies while emphasizing the patients' thinking patterns as well as actions. In the same way that certain behaviors are automatically provoked under given conditions, well-ingrained thoughts are repeatedly triggered when presented with familiar cues.

Familiar thought patterns link to other thoughts in a kind of "cognitive chain" with self-defeating cycles being reinforced every time certain links of the chain are activated. Those thoughts then provoke familiar (but often disturbing) emotions – such as anxiety or depression. By learning to re-direct one's thoughts earlier in the chain and replace them with positive patterns, the cycles can be stopped. Habitual unpleasant emotions should then be less readily accessible.

We are chronically reinforcing destructive habits every time negative thoughts activate emotional responses that tap familiar and equally destructive thoughts. Within seconds, a person prone to depression can lose every shred of hope – although it probably *seems* like a dark cloud that just appeared from nowhere. Learning to recognize how our thinking contributes to (or causes) surges of disturbing emotions is a very useful tool.

Psychodynamic Therapy

To most people, therapy means *talk therapy*, conjuring up stereotypes from movies and television – a little Freud, a few dreams, tearful patients with low self-esteem, sexual secrets, and crippling fears that amazingly disappear once they 1) remember being traumatically abused in a horrific sacrificial manner; or 2) realize they always secretly hated (or lusted for) their parents. Those parodies say little about how psychotherapy can actually heal, or about the real interactions that occur in a session room.

Psychodynamic Therapy has become a catch-phrase encompassing analytic-based, supportive, expressive, and eclectic approaches. More specifically, everything from Freudian or Jungian to Supportive Therapy, Analytic-based (with further differences such as Object Relations, Ego-Psychology, Self-Psychology) fall under this umbrella.

Psychodynamic therapies are based on the premise that the more we know about *why* and *how* we do what we do, the greater our capacity to change.

Self-knowledge comes from connecting memories to current behaviors and feelings, and searching for patterns of faulty beliefs that have become ingrained. Links are made between recurring problems and the basic convictions we hold (which may or may not be true). Events leading up to symptom development point to where and how the system began to break down.

This is not about blaming the patient's past. In fact, contrary to how we feel, self-defeating beliefs (and repeated behaviors) are not the result of anything that happened *to* us. We become who we are as a result of *interpretations* we made in response to events, and convictions we developed, habits that stuck and world-views that, over time, became *integrated* into the core of basic character.

How did we put things together? What sweeping generalizations were made based on our experiences, and how are we hurting ourselves by not re-examining early convictions? Is it even possible to revise a view of the past so significantly that we actually change ourselves in the present?

- **Supportive therapy** (once or twice a week, possibly even less) is different from other psychodynamic approaches in that it can be *directive* – including at least a modicum of practical advice from the therapist. The emphasis is on helping the patient to *sustain* and *improve basic functioning* rather than searching deeper for clues and links to the *whys* of behavior. In the "depth" therapies (delving deeper into unconscious motivations) a patient may experience periodic increases in anxiety levels. When/if patients doubt their current strength to tolerate more anxious arousal, treatment focuses on gaining the understanding needed for daily coping without encouraging any regression or transference (defined under analytic-based therapy).

- **Expressive therapy** (two or three times a week) goes to the depths that Supportive only skims. This is almost guaranteed to be a longer-term treatment, and requires fortitude on the part of the patient. Likely to be also be called Analytic-based and/or Depth-therapy, sessions revolve around the patient's free associations, memories, and self-identity with emphasis on the dynamic between patient and therapist. When it works, depth-therapies can make permanent changes within very stubborn problems – and the knowledge gained is valuable for a lifetime.

In general, psychodynamic therapies focus on the whole person – with relief from symptoms being a by-product of the exploration of thoughts, feelings, beliefs and defenses.

The *depth-therapies* (analytic-based) consider symptoms to be *clues* for underlying conflicts, rather than signs of an illness. With that approach:
1) treatment will not be quick;
2) although it is important to describe the symptoms that bring us into therapy, most patients (myself included) keep talking *only* about that bundle of bad symptoms. There is the unspoken belief that we are coming to sessions in order to explain our bad mental state as clearly and in as much detail as possible. *If we finally tell it **right**, the doctor will heal us*. The therapist has a different agenda – and will be looking for *metaphorical* connections between those symptoms and other areas of thinking, personality and ingrained traits. Patients not prepared for this approach may feel misunderstood.

In this regard, targeting the underlying symptom has an important meaning. It may be that what we have identified as our entire package of symptoms (the anxiety, depression, obsessions, panic, etc.) are collectively *responses* to other symptoms that we may not even recognize as problematic at all. They may have existed for years in the form of traits, and have become intrinsic to us, i.e., ego-syntonic. Some of those character traits and coping mechanisms are very likely the underlying symptoms that actually caused the breakdown. If so, problems in those areas need to be resolved in order to stop the production of *resulting* symptoms (anxiety, depression, etc.) and prevent their reoccurrence.

Pyschoanalytic-Based Therapy

This is the treatment approach that worked for me, and I admit to prejudice in favor of it. However, it is not my intent to push analytic therapy as a choice over other valid treatments - only to describe some useful concepts for readers who might not otherwise be exposed to them. [The reader should know that there is more than one type of "psychoanalytic treatment." Within the field, several major divisions - Freudian drive theory, Ego Psychology, Object Relations and Self-Psychology – each interpret human development and mental processes from a different core theory and therefore define treatment goals and techniques differently. Discussions in this book do not cover these distinctions, and anyone seriously interested in pursuing an analytic-based treatment may want to explore them elsewhere].

While much of our mental processes occur with full awareness, an even greater part happens "off-stage" – in the unconscious. Actions and feelings that seem to contradict what we say we want probably arise from unacknowledged agendas within our minds. What we label as our "reasons" may be after-the-fact justifications created to fool ourselves into believing we were fully aware of our motivations and desires. The goal of treatment is greater self-understanding, and the elimination of symptoms is a by-product of a healthier, sturdier self.

Making the unconscious *conscious*, increases our abilities to:

Revise our sense of self and personal view of the past;
Explore potent conflicts;
Put words to unacknowledged thoughts.

Transference *is the process of relating to people and current situations as if they are actually old relationships and events (especially those based on significant childhood relationships with parents, etc.).*

When enmeshed in transference, we expect everyone to fall into a few rigid stereotypes, believing *"that's the way people are."* Instead of reacting to the unfamiliar, we assign old roles to new faces based on a stable of (unconscious and automatic) memories. We are not necessarily reliving past relationships because they were pleasant, only because they are familiar. Our abilities to cope with them (and therefore with others like them) are already proven. The past represents a battle we know we can survive. Time and again, the devil we know is chosen over a stranger.

One hallmark of this treatment is the extensive work done on transference. If other therapies serve as *lectures* on why we act and feel the way we do, then analytic treatment is the *lab*. The interactions between patient and therapist serve as a canvas, displaying the strategies at work in the patient's mind. Our responses to our own thoughts and feelings basically define who we are, and operate outside the realm of self-observation. The coping strategies we use, and the behaviors we consistently employ in relationships will appear in real time and living color in the relationship with the therapist. It affords a front row seat (with guided commentary) into the way our minds actually work.

With transference, every similarity between past and present is magnified – and every difference between *then* and *now* is minimized. By the time we finish revising a current situation to feel familiar, we see precisely what we expected to see. The amount of reality lost in that process is not small.

PARIS IN THE
THE SPRING

What does that title say? (are you sure? Read it again)

Seeing what we expect to see is the result of automatic actions, not conscious choices. The type of memory that creates and maintains transference is an *unconscious* recall – habits so deeply ingrained that we fail to recognize them as conditioned. In the midst of repeating the past, we feel sure that our assessments are accurate and impartial observations of what we see in front of us. But implicit memory is dictating them from outside awareness. And we have no idea that what we "see" is more about what we *remember*.

When treatment works, those repetitions are interrupted and eventually made conscious, allowing the doctor/patient relationship to develop into a new type of experience, consisting of who the two people actually *are*. In fact, it may be the patient's first close relationship that is *not* transferential.

> *Admittedly, it may be hard to see what any of this has to do with symptoms. We enter therapy because we are suffering - and thinking only about how to stop anxiety or depression or depersonalization. It can seem absurd to spend time examining the ways we relate to people.*
>
> *But in order to keep re-experiencing the past in the present, we unknowingly foster a kind of self- stagnation. Over time, it becomes a resistance to growth, a morbid fear of anything unexpected. We monitor every feeling, trying to anticipate what might be felt or thought before it can be felt or thought. Eventually, we are left with a **phobia of internal change**. When staying the same becomes both essential and impossible, that paradox will provoke a breakdown.*

Towards Understanding The Mind

*CHAPTER NOTE: This chapter offers more information than any breakdown sufferer will ever need. It is for the highly curious reader who enjoys psychological theory. Throughout my illness, I searched for books to help me understand **how** unconscious thoughts could create something as bizarre and disturbing as my symptoms. Most of the material was written for mental health professionals and students – requiring a background of extensive knowledge. This chapter is the layperson's overview that I kept looking for, but never found.*

We know something that we doubt any normal person will ever understand. We are more than scared or sad. Something has changed inside of us. When people try to help, we play along – pretending that our fears are *"a case of bad nerves"* or that loss of self is *"feeling depressed."* Secretly, we are convinced it is beyond anxiety or depression because no matter what anyone says, we believe that something has happened to the very way we **think**. And we are absolutely right.

However, it is not insanity or brain damage. Instead, we have shifted into a kind of thought process that humans rarely access during ordinary daily life.

A mental breakdown is a form of regression (the mind reverts to experiencing emotions and fantasies that might belong to a very young child, and most importantly – will experience them in the same *way* a child processes thoughts and feelings). It is a return to the thought construction of Primary Process – the style of thinking used by the unconscious – and the way our minds create dreams. Consider how radically different a dream experience feels from thoughts in waking life – that is the same degree of disparity between primary and secondary (normal consciousness) thought. And that is the disparity between your ordinary state of mind and the new experience this breakdown has created.

Understanding how primary process differs from ordinary consciousness offers insight into the way a breakdown temporarily alters our thinking and sense of identity – and why it feels unquestionably like madness.

How Could Any Normal Brain Be Doing This?

That question consumed me. Without an answer, how would I ever trust that my brain wasn't damaged, or that the breakdown was not the beginning of deterioration?

"Those are only symptoms of stress."
*BUT: I had been **much** more stressed at other times in life without any problems at all.*

"You seem to be in a constant state of anxiety – and that is causing your peculiar feelings."
BUT: Yes, NOW I'm in a constant state of anxiety – but I was never like this before the breakdown!

"What you're feeling is a response to disturbing hidden thoughts."
BUT: If I have such thoughts, surely I've always had them – why did all hell break loose <u>now</u>? Also, how horrific must they be if they can make me believe I'm going insane??

A DIFFERENT KIND OF THINKING

Human thoughts are produced both consciously and unconsciously (termed Secondary and Primary Process, respectively). Thoughts created through Primary Process have qualities that are remarkably different from consciousness. They possess a surreal, almost *Alice in Wonderland* tone – defying logic, discounting reality and ignoring laws of time and space. Although nothing could *feel* more "crazy", primary process is actually a perfectly normal function of a healthy mind. But it can be highly disorienting when it dominates our perceptions unexpectedly and seemingly at random -- as if in the middle of an average day, you suddenly entered a dream state.

In The Language Of Symptoms - Condensation & Displacement

Both breakdown symptoms and dreams are painted by the same artist – using two signature strokes that are unmistakable. Recognizing them and how they function are keys to deconstructing hidden meanings behind symptoms (and dreams).

Consider the familiar statements:
 "*...but I can't see what these awful feelings have to do with anything going on in my life!*" or "*I was just calmly walking down the street, and had an anxiety attack out of nowhere – I wasn't thinking or doing anything to bring it on!*"

Condensation operates like highly efficient mental shorthand. It is a feature of thought construction that takes numerous powerful ideas, wishes, fears, etc. and packs their meanings into a **single symbol**. In addition, parts of an idea may stand for the whole (and vice versa).

The result is that one panic attack can represent several frightening thoughts – but those thoughts/ideas may not seem related to each other. This is so foreign to the way conscious mind assimilates and assigns connections that we cannot envision it as *system* at all. We incorrectly assume our symptoms must be linked to fears, ideas, etc. in very logical ways. If I suddenly feel anxious, there must be something right here in front of me making me fearful (or at least a single thought right here in front of my mind that is very disturbing). During conscious remembering, we chunk ideas according to a chronology and/or link them by shared emotional content. Seeing a bloody scene in a movie may remind me of my own leg injury when I was a child - which may in turn make me remember a happier scene from that same summer. But the memory of one's first kiss does not get "filed" with Aunt Susan's cheesecake recipe and the bloody leg and the total amount due on last year's tax refund. Consciousness dictates that thoughts belong together only if they have some logically significant features in common.

But condensation operates *unconsciously* – where no such logic is required. Separate memories of grief, sexual arousal, terror and inhibition can be encapsulated within the same symbol.

In the normal realm, that is partly why art holds such power over our emotions. We respond to numerous visceral stimuli within a single image, and the resulting feeling of being emotionally swept away is a mild (and enjoyable) form of induced regression.

Displacement: To further disguise meaning, a strong emotional response to someone or something can be **reassigned** to a seemingly unrelated person or object. Displacement is a mental construct that often makes dream interpretation seem far-fetched. Example: displacement might allow a waking-life argument with a spouse to appear within the dream in the form of a fight with an office co-worker. But to make matters fuzzier, it might not show up as a fight at all – but as a benign interaction with some other person. The "*point*" to any dream can be located in one small detail within the tableau of a complex image. The dream's more obvious storyline and dramatic actions may be camouflage. (and remember, the same is true for the origin of symptoms).

In the above example, presume the woman's last argument with her husband struck a frightening chord in her because she fears that if she gets too angry, one of them will lose control and literally end the marriage. In her own words "*I need to keep a lid on it or who knows what might happen.*" The resulting dream: image of the husband in the midst of a jovial carnival scene – filled with distractions – all subterfuge for one meaningful symbol that stands for her hidden fear – nearby but unnoticed by the crowd, a lion paces in its cage – a cage with a lock that is missing.

Phobias are often the product of displacement. That dreaded spider or airplane or tightly-enclosed space represents a completely different threatening idea – and we convince ourselves that by avoiding our phobia object, we are containing a seemingly unrelated thought. None of this is conscious, of course – all we know is that we feel close to dying when that plane takes off.

Symptoms and dreams cannot be taken at face value. While a single thought may trigger an anxiety attack, it might be so well-disguised that any conscious thoughts immediately prior will bear no resemblance to the idea represented in the symptom. So when we insist *"I was just window shopping – I wasn't thinking anything disturbing!"* – we are both right and wrong. *Consciously*, we had no disturbing thoughts. That is only half the equation.

Distinguishing between Primary and Secondary Process

Secondary Process thinking needs no description. It is everything you consider *thinking* to be. It is logical and intentional. It uses language as a tool for communication. It is the mental process I use when choosing these words, and the process you use to read them. If you put the book down and think about its content, that is still Secondary Process. Nearly any thinking you do *on purpose* falls in this category. Secondary Process is:

- Rational and linear.
- In human development, it evolves as we master language. Secondary Process allows us to comprehend abstract meanings (to use the alphabet as building blocks where words represent symbols for ideas, etc.). Over time, our ability to use language actually determines the way we think. Even when not speaking or writing, we create thoughts in "logical order" – according to the syntax of whatever language we predominantly use. Point is: while that kind of thinking feels innately *logical*, it is actually a learned skill.
- Follows the rules of physical reality (presumes concepts such as cause/effect, time, sequence – beginning, middle, end, later, earlier, etc.)

Descriptions of conscious thought are so obvious they hardly need stating. But they establish a contrast to primary process - where nothing logical or obvious can be taken for granted.

Primary Process:

- creates meaning in images rather than words;
- **condenses** numerous (and seemingly unrelated) ideas into a single symbol;
- **displaces** its objects/targets. A forbidden thought about kissing Jim may emerge in a dream as two strangers kissing *in a gym (don't look to primary process for dazzling wit. It is economical, childish and primitive. Think "knock-knock" jokes);*
- often uses an opposite to indicate meaning;
- disregards the laws of physical reality;
- creates thoughts outside the boundaries of time (no concept of sequence, or past, present, future). Impulses/drives exist only in the present moment – memory is re-experienced rather than recalled. Needs demand satisfaction right now;
- ignores the meanings of "not" or "no" - or any form of negated idea. In the language of primary process, "I do not love him" means the same as "I love him" Everything IS (ignores negatives), and everything is NOW (ignores time and sequence). [This is an important symptom-related concept – telling yourself *not* to feel or think a certain way is actually reinforcing the symptom. The regressed mind processes only the idea, ignoring your negation].
- Example: the kind of thinking used in dreams

Symptoms created in Primary Process will possess qualities that logical mind cannot fathom.

If primary process seems too bizarre to grasp, imagine playing a game of charades (or even closer, a game of *Pictionary*). Clearly, you are not going to act out the entire movie *The Matrix*, but instead will break down the title into segments. Doing a pantomime (or drawing) of pulling a bunny out of a hat (*magic **trick***) invites your teammates to zero in on the word "*trick*" which can easily be stretched into "*tricks*" plural – then you might enact a person falling asleep to inspire a guess of "*night*" which can easily be **reversed** to evoke the word "*day*." If the players repeat "*The day-tricks*" they may soon hear "*The Matrix*" and win that round of the game. We "think differently" when playing such games, and we abandon logic for symbolic efficiency.

In the Language of Dreams

With no regard for reality, a dreamer steps on an elevator and emerges into a playground from childhood. Faces suddenly morph into other faces, or vanish without excuse or explanation. And as participants, we accept all of it as falling within the parameters of "dream rules" -- because during a dream the *effects created by primary process* are being experienced while we are still *thinking* in primary process. But trying to filter those surreal concepts through ordinary awareness creates a feeling of losing reality.

Unconscious thoughts consist mostly of images. Not dialogue or stories or logical ideas. And when words are used, they function very differently than the conscious mind would expect. A word rarely means its dictionary definition. Instead, the way it *sounds* can be a clue – or the visual effects of its letters arranged in a pattern. Rhymes, puns and picture puzzles are the stuff of Primary Process. It is a kind of code, but a very simple one. Look for the most literal and unsophisticated meaning.

I might use the image of a large eyeball to represent *myself* (eye = "I"). I might imagine standing beneath your window as an expression of "*I understand you.*" ("*I am standing **under** you*"). Very corny, a little trite. That is the Unconscious.

Therapists often suggest these kinds of hidden meanings to a patient's symptoms, because they are searching for clues that resonate within primary process. If unfamiliar with these ideas, you may be appalled at the therapist's simplicity.

Patient: *The sun is so bright today – it's almost blinding.*
Therapist: *What might you not want to 'see' right now?* (or looking for the opposite* (another way of denying negation) – "*what are you afraid you're not able to look at directly or face?*" It can certainly sound lame. But that is exactly the way primary process creates meaning.

* Remember the example of playing *charades* or *Pictionary*. It is often easier (more efficient) to act out the *opposite* of a word that you want your teammates to guess – then a gesture to communicate "reverse it" is simple and quick.

The unconscious uses opposites in similar ways. Often we can allow ourselves the conscious recognition of a dangerous idea

only by thinking its *opposite* – we feel safe because the idea is still being denied, but can alleviate pressing anxiety by giving it *some* form of expression - even if only after negating it.

Why Primary Process Dominates A Breakdown

The Power of Unconscious Thoughts

Conscious thoughts and worries (those we are fully aware of) can be highly disturbing. They keep us awake at night and torment us throughout the day. But they are rarely the stuff of breakdowns. Likewise, thoughts that have been exiled to the unconscious pose little threat. There they operate *behind the scenes* without forcing the mind to acknowledge anything that could challenge its status quo.

Breakdown symptoms can be triggered by unacceptable thoughts that reside in the middle – dangerously close to awareness, but still unacknowledged. The potential acknowledgment (or the conflict between *to acknowledge or not to acknowledge*) produces strong anxiety – which soon cascades into symptom-responses.

Forget everything you know from TV-movies about repressed memories – horrifying flash-backs of sexual or ritual abuse. There is probably nothing shocking about your 'dangerous' thought. In order to sound alarms, it only needs to radically contradict other tightly-held beliefs. The mind takes drastic steps to prevent such thoughts from expression, not only if they are ghastly, but when they could challenge beliefs we consider essential to self-cohesion.

For this example, grant that Premises A & B are true (and must remain true according to my tightly held self-image):
 Premise A: *I never get angry at a person I love;*
 Premise B: *I love Person Y.*

Any anger I feel towards Person Y creates a conundrum. How can those two contradictory truths co-exist? I am clutching at two essential beliefs that conflict with each other completely. Something has got to give. If I cannot adjust my belief system, then what *gives* may be my mental stability.

If the anger I feel at Person Y remains unconscious (allowing me to plod along happily with my unacknowledged paradox), I feel safe. The moment it comes closer to conscious awareness, alarms will sound. The thought demands expression – ideally in words, but my mind is trying hard to deny it a voice. (By the way, that is largely how the depth-therapies work. The patient is able to find words for ideas that were demanding expression – detonating their power by finally bringing them out of primary process experience).

In the meantime, a compromise may allow the thought *partial* expression – in the form of a symptom. That symptom is created to be a coded version of the hidden idea – serving as appeasement of a powerful and dangerous thought that we remain unable to hear.

That thought/symptom hybrid is destined to be experienced partially in consciousness and partially through the bizarre language of the unconscious. Half-real, half-fantasy. Part dream state/part reality. To know and not know simultaneously. The symptom may be born through a kind of *Alice in Wonderland* illogical logic – deductive reasoning that is technically accurate (the integrity of the premises are retained), but capable of producing some weird conclusions by ignoring the laws of reality. In the example above:

I never get angry at a person I love;
I love Person Y.

Unbounded by rules of reality, the unconscious can solve my paradox without missing a beat:

If I hold it true that I am someone who loves Person Y, and also that I am someone who cannot be angry at anyone I love, then a viable solution is:

Conclusion (courtesy of primary process) = *I am no longer me.*

The result is a depersonalization symptom (as symbolic *expression* of dangerous thoughts). It is a literal feeling of unreality, a sudden and terrifying sensation of losing oneself. This is not mental abstraction, but a primitive *experience* – I actually *feel* I am literally no longer me. I may develop massive anxiety along with it, or a panic attack. I may imagine myself falling away from reality as if my mind suddenly imploded. I am experiencing a thought that my mind is not yet willing or able to intellectually acknowledge.

The abstract thought *"then I am no longer me"* is not an insane idea. If that same sequence of logic could be interpreted through conscious thinking, the *metaphorical* truth of its conclusion would be clear i.e., *perhaps I am not the "me" I always believed I was.* And that idea could be examined intellectually, without needing to be experienced. But for that to happen, I would expose a rather large flaw in one of my two original premises. Unable to acknowledge that yet, I keep the sophisticated concept of *"am I the me I always thought I was?"* out of awareness – and in its place, I experience its primitive translation as a partial reality.

Bear in mind that we are unaware of the content of thoughts causing symptoms. This theory is not blaming us for our condition, i.e., suggesting we would rather hide from thoughts than get well. We are not intentionally holding onto symptoms. But we may have been avoiding so *much* -- so *well* -- for so *long* -- that many thoughts seem to not exist. It is when they come very close to awareness that the symptom spiral begins.

>We are being fooled by our own minds.
>We do not realize what is causing our pain.
>We are totally unaware that any conflict exists.

A Few Misconceptions about the Unconscious

In writing about the mind, accuracy gets sacrificed for imagery: "*pushing thoughts down into the unconscious....*or *ideas rising from outside awareness and entering consciousness...* " as if those are actual locations in the brain. Thoughts exist as conscious or unconscious based on the type of mental energy they contain, not because they are *in* unconsciousness, or move *into* consciousness. The unconscious is not a *chamber* that hides forbidden wishes and memories. Rather than a place, imagine it as a **process of thinking**. It is a method of expressing thoughts using a very different "language" from its counterpart. Taboo wishes/memories are not physically hidden anywhere, but have been encoded into a style of thinking that is not recognized by consciousness.

Conscious and unconscious thoughts are active and interdependent. Together they form a kind of mental tango, alternating in dominance, and functioning in complement to each other with polar tension.

Far from dormant or passive, unconscious thoughts participate non-stop in the brain's activities – within the system that transmits fears, wishes and impulses, and constantly links to conscious thoughts, retrieves memories, communicates needs, and seeks relief from tension. We are at the *effect* of our unconscious thoughts; we are just not aware of their actual content (and therefore need not integrate them into our sense of reality and self).

On the contrary, conscious thought production occasionally shuts down i.e., whenever we are *no longer conscious* (during sleep, under anesthesia, in hypnotic states, etc.). At those times, the unconscious temporarily achieves dominance and its *surreal* qualities become the most obvious – in the language of dreams, fantasies, delusions, slips of the tongue, and symptoms.

Another misconception is that only the unconscious holds *truth* (what we really want and intend), with the implication that conscious thoughts are all self-deceptive. It is not that simple. Granted, unconscious thoughts are not distorted by the censorship of conscious mind, and in that sense, are more pure. But conscious and unconscious function like a figure/ground drawing. Together they form the boundary or frame that mutually defines them. Both are *constantly present,* just not "seen" simultaneously.

Finding Meaning Within symptoms

Depersonalization/derealization states provide good examples of how a symptom may serve as metaphor for unexpressed thoughts.

"*This cannot be happening to me*" – is a partially-conscious idea common to trauma victims. It may accompany a feeling of unreality, depersonalization or déjà vu (the phenomenon that gives us an eerie sense of familiarity in brand new situations, i.e., the feeling that I have lived this moment before, or that I seem to *recognize* a place or person that I never saw before this very moment). The mind literally creates an experience of denying the reality of events in front of us. And this type of defensive reaction operates not only under severe circumstances of violence or terror, but also in response to disturbing ideas of a much more ordinary nature.

A thought looms close to awareness that, if brought into consciousness, would pose massive threat to another highly valued belief(s). The mind acknowledges potential danger. The thought must be stopped. However, it is pushing for expression – and will continue to provoke anxiety until it finds release.

Example 1: *I can count on my brother more than anyone else I know. I am so admiring of him that he can literally do no wrong in my eyes. Lately, however, he has been acting different. I try to ignore it, or chalk it up to some new romance or work problem, but I am starting to see something about him that I'd never seen before.* **If my observations are correct, then maybe he is different than I've always believed.** That new suspicion is not conscious for me, however. Consciously, I am only concerned about him and want to do whatever I can to help. Below consciousness, I am absorbing more disturbing realities about him – that he is far from perfect and far from unselfish. Those are thoughts I do not want to know, yet thoughts that are becoming harder and harder not to see.

The dangerous ideas hovering near awareness might be: *How could I not have realized what he's really like? He has a side to him that is infuriating. I can't face this realization, because I've always needed to see him as perfect. It is also frightening to imagine that if he, this man I thought I knew so well, is not who I've always thought he was, maybe the same is true for me.* My sense of security is under attack, even my feeling of constancy about who I am. Under the right circumstances, with the right amount of emotions invested, that series of thoughts could sound a danger signal.

The concept represented by the idea "*my brother seems like a different person today*" is too threatening to be absorbed into awareness. One way to keep it hidden and yet discharge some of the tension it creates is to express the thought in the language of primary process. The result is a state of derealization.

This regressed state of mind causes me to partially *experience* what a higher level of thinking would only *symbolize*. Depersonalization can result from an "as if" metaphor that is processed as reality.

At that moment, I register awareness of my brother as if he is no longer himself – to my mind's eye, not an hallucination. *I can literally recognize him, but the experience of what I see has shifted. Soon nothing around me looks right, other people's faces are distorted as well... my family no longer looks familiar. Anxiety mounts, and I begin doubting my own sanity. It feels like I've secretly been given LSD, and absurd as that is, I start wondering if anyone could have slipped a drug into my food. Within minutes, I'm in total panic, trying to "force" people to look right. I stare at the details of their faces, trying to reorient – of course, I make matters worse by hyper-focusing. I feel like I'm in a dream, or under water.*

That progression of bizarre feelings is the result of a metaphor ("my brother seems like a different person") being expressed in the form of a symptom.

Since this experience is unlike anything in logical mind, I lack language to even describe how it feels. It is a delusion, but not a delusion. The more I search for words, the more I realize how insane I must sound. But efforts at talking myself back into normal thinking are doomed to fail because I am trying to apply *secondary* process reasoning to an experience that was created outside the jurisdiction of logic.

In summary: To protect the self's status quo, a dangerous thought was exiled. Then as external factors (life events, behaviors of others, etc.) provoked its expression, the thought began teasing the surface of awareness. The closer it got, the more anxiety it produced. The longer the thought was denied (while close to awareness), the more it sought expression – which continued to increase tension. As long as the thought remained *outside* awareness, the vehicle for its expression was primary process - where it could find no outlet in words, but through a kind of experienced metaphor. It creates a voice at a very high cost to the mind – finding expression in the form of a depersonalization symptom.

If you are consumed by the same fears, worries and obsessions every day – and each time find them as disturbing as the first - you might feel guilty or embarrassed for not being able to "talk yourself out of it." People around you may keep asking why reason and logic are of so little help.

We *know* we are experiencing an altered state of consciousness. We know we are not in danger. We *know* our perceptions are highly sensitive. We *know* we did not lose control (or sanity) the other 50 times, so we will likely survive this episode, too. We know all those things. But in the domain of primary process, knowledge is barely a band-aid.

Remember: this is not a sign of weakness – or stubbornness -- or negativity – or lack of will power. You are being fooled by the *master* of illusion – your own unconscious.

This is not to imply that every episode of depersonalization (or other symptoms) will be the direct result of an unwanted thought. Once an altered state of consciousness has been accessed repeatedly, it becomes a "room" that is easy to enter. After a breakdown, the slightest threat to status quo will re-invoke symptoms. Remember the earlier analogy of an anxious robbery victim who waits nightly for the next invasion. The tension of the waiting and the hyper-alertness of his remembered fear will eventually force him to act – and he sends the attack dogs on the heels of an "intruder" who turns out to be the mailman.

A Dangerous Patient

Below is a description of a patient as seen from a consulting doctor's perspective. Imagine you have been asked to read the doctor's notes and further evaluate this patient's prognosis, severity of disorder and appropriate treatment.

As you read, look for symptoms, traits, signs of reality testing, etc.

Patient A – emotionally volatile, goes from extreme rage to joy (including loud laughter) within seconds. Often has nightmares that prevent returning to sleep, and is prone to intermittent paranoia involving fears that someone or something is "waiting" to harm her in the next room. She can usually be talked into a reconnection with reality, but silent delusions persist that center around "ghosts" and other magical ideas. There appears to be a connection between these episodes and darkness – reality testing is improved during the day, but returns in the night hours without provocation

Patient can be charming and responsive with evidence of strong communication skills, but on-going relatedness is interrupted by sudden demands, displays of aggression and loud vocalized despair. Although not believed to be dangerous, the patient requires vigilant observation to prevent her from potentially harming *herself*.

While speaking, she becomes highly impatient if her listeners attempt to redirect their attention in the slightest – and on several occasions has shown uncontrolled aggression in response.

— A Dangerous Patient —

Despite frequent sociability, patient must be placed in isolation when bodily responses such as fatigue, hunger, or discomfort provoke intense frustration. At those times, patient loses the ability to restrain her own impulses, and if left in an over-stimulating environment, may berate others or destroy her own possessions.

Does this patient seem severely ill? Can you imagine treating her and how difficult it might be?

Actually, she is not ill at all. Her "disturbances" are explained by one fact: she is two years old. Like all toddlers, she is demanding, delusional, jealous, irrational, seductive and violent. The psyches of small children are very dark. They have too much to absorb, and too little maturity to file it away. Their own emotions terrify them – as evidenced in nightmares filled with destruction – and fantasies of monsters eating them alive. The early authors of fairy tales knew it -- Hansel's pending doom in the witch's oven, Snow White's naïve bite into poison fruit. Those stories mirror a child's wild emotions and confusion over adult behavior.

Those fairy tales, just like the child's thinking, are woven in *black and white*. There is good and there is evil, nothing in between. There are monsters and angels, no middle ground. There is eternal safety or terror, but no steps on a spectrum. "Happily-ever-after" or being devoured by a giant. A child's defenses are built on extremes. And every adult still harbors a 2 yr. old self – although with development, we no longer rely on that defensive inner world.

But when poor and outdated defenses operate too often, we get stuck in time – trapped by obsolete strategies that continue to make us respond without full use of conscious thinking. We are at the effect of an emotional control panel that activates alarms unnecessarily – and fails to sound in situations that merit them.

The peculiarities of primary process are easy to spot in a small child's thinking. This is probably the dominant form of thought production before language is mastered.

Calmly announce to an unsuspecting 2-year old "*by the way, there is no ice cream*" and you know what comes next: immediate demands for (non-existent) ice cream. The "no" cannot hold a candle to the immediate desire that was activated in the child's mind. And modifying your original statement to "*but there will be some ice cream tonight*" still brings little peace. Time is always *now* because the *impulse* is now. The abstractions of sequence, negation, and past/present/future is a sophisticated level of thinking that takes years to develop. Until then, just don't say '*ice cream*' if you don't want to start something. Within that analogy, merely *having a thought* can spur a threatening impulse that is equally powerful and immune to logic – as long as the thought continues to be experienced through primary process. "*No*" doesn't count. Time and sequence are meaningless.

If you have a recurring fear of losing control, trying to reassure yourself with counteractive thoughts such as "*but I will not lose control, I will not do anything horrible...*" will fall on deaf ears. You might as well tell yourself "I *would* do it" because that is precisely what the unconscious registers. Attempting to negate a fear may enhance its intensity.

A clearer example is to imagine lying in bed and repeating over and over before you fall asleep "*I will not dream about the office tonight.*" Those repetitions will be heard as a "suggestion" to the unconscious – and chances are good you just talked yourself *into* a dream about the office.

This does not mean that you will talk yourself into losing control! The point is that you may very well enhance your *fear* of it by reinforcing the idea in the deeper recesses of your thinking.

Remember the two-year old. If you want to take her mind off ice cream, *distract* her rather than trying to convince her to *not think* about it.

DEFENSES

"I'm not using my symptoms as a defense!"

The word itself makes people defensive, because the term is usually misunderstood. **Psychological Defenses** operate in everyone's mind. They are not signs of pathology or weakness. They are essential for healthy adaptive experience. Normally, potentially disturbing thoughts are kept out of awareness through the use of effective defenses. The effective ones work in conjunction with a mature self, while others (called *lower-level*) are remnants from earlier development. Faulty defenses can create more problems than they solve.

High-level defenses operate in conjunction within sophisticated thinking (secondary process thought). Low-level defenses presume a reality that is far from accurate. Developed when the mind was functioning in primary process (at a *very* young age), low-level defenses were created to protect a self who was not yet clearly defined from other people, and who lived in a world of absolutes (black & white rather than shades of gray). The result is a set of defenses that do nothing to promote growth, mastery or maturity, and in fact, reinforce poor reality testing every time they are called to action.

Higher Level Defenses include:

Repression: Disturbing thoughts are removed from consciousness and **encoded into** primary process. It is as if the dangerous thought has been exiled and no longer poses a threat to awareness. However, the thought has not been annihilated. It continues to exist as a factor in the mind, and can impact other thoughts it links to at any given time. When this defense works, it is very effective.

Sublimation: troublesome thoughts/feelings are **redirected** into acceptable forms of expression. The thought is no longer consciously perceived as a threat once it finds an outlet, because it has been 'changed' into something the mind perceives as acceptable. It is expressed and denied simultaneously.

> *Notice how often that theme recurs – the duality of knowing and not knowing or of simultaneously expressing and hiding. Understanding duality and the role it plays in breakdown symptoms can be useful.*

Anger might be channeled into an obsession with ice hockey; exhibitionism inspires a career in the theater. Those are ridiculously obvious, but some inventive and well-disguised forms of sublimation are described in the following section.

All defenses are *designed* by our own minds and in *service* of our own minds – protecting us from disturbing thoughts that also arise *within our own minds*. If that sounds absurdly complicated, it should – the process is a mental trick requiring masterful self-deception. The mind literally finds ways to both know and not know something - at the same time - and accomplishes this feat without sacrificing sanity.

What do Defenses protect us from?
Our own thoughts (those that if made conscious, would produce painful or frightening feelings by destroying our sense of safety and control).

What kinds of thoughts are that dangerous?
There are unbearable aspects to reality. In order to function, we control how much reality (and which parts) register at a given time.

Thoughts that must be warded off include those:
1. *Too terrifying to accept (death, powerlessness)*
2. *Too provocative to restrain;*
3. *Too contradictory to integrate into one's self-image.*

1. Thoughts too terrifying to accept:
Human existence is precarious. We must find ways to care about life's details while knowing we may not survive till nightfall. Will something horrible happen to us? To our loved ones? Will the people we need keep loving us? Or if alone, will we always be? And regardless of good fortune, the entire show is destined to close – we live every minute with irrefutable evidence that we are headed for death. (Is the reader feeling better, yet?)

No mind could maintain stability if it embraced the truth about its condition with constant awareness. So we fool ourselves much of the time – we make plans as if we know we will still be alive tomorrow. We invest tremendous energy and passion in other equally fragile humans. We proceed as if we are *much* more secure than we probably are.

Then on top of it, we must include rational precautions – avoiding danger as best we can and being prepared for needs arising overnight. We are striving for enough reality to keep our choices sensible, and enough fantasy to make them pleasurable.

Good defenses accomplish that. Poor defenses can make matters worse.

<u>Important</u>: all defenses operate unconsciously. We can see evidence that we use them, and which ones we seem to use the most, but we are unaware of the process while it takes place. This is significant, because unconscious maneuvers are very difficult to change. To change or replace a defense requires locating the thoughts that repeatedly provoke it into action. But it took time to develop our coping mechanisms, and it takes time to change them. Any promise of a quick fix involving the unconscious will be equally short-lived in how long the solution lasts.

2. Thoughts too provocative to contain (aggressive and sexual impulses):

Those two powerful human drives are constantly pulling us towards action. They are primitive – linked to instincts - making them even stronger as each thought is quickly supported by biological responses.

While being tugged, the more sophisticated parts of our mind are assessing how any such action might affect our:
>Social acceptability(how <u>others</u> will assess me)
>Long term best interests
>Self-image- integrity/values (how I assess myself)

Most sexual and aggressive impulses would never make it past that checkpoint. But to constantly police those drives would be like spending a day in a china shop with a two-year old.
"No!" "no, no....no!" "don't touch that..." "come over here.." "no, not that either, no..."

If a two year old is told not to touch the glass ball, she will not extrapolate that she probably shouldn't touch the glass *horse* either. Each impulse must be curbed one by one…by one…by one. It would require a staggering amount of energy from conscious mind.

Instead, (unconscious) defenses re-channel strong drives into acceptable forms of expression. The underlying motives may easy to figure out – the performing artist who channels exhibitionism. But exhibitionism could also be the motive for a teaching career – rather than the teacher's *conscious* reason of wanting to help others (an additional motivation, just not exclusively). Likewise, a surgeon may admit to omnipotent fantasies about mastery over death, but be unaware that those daily encounters with scalpels, blood and pain could be satisfying (unconscious) sadistic aggression.

In each case, a defense took powerful (unacceptable) drives and re-directed them into productive and satisfying activities. When **sublimation** works, it rarely matters if we see our original motive/satisfaction involved.

Lower Level defenses cause the problems. They close down large areas of thinking and require complex detours. "Lower" level here meaning primitive, archaic - mechanisms developed while very young and not replaced over time.
Defenses set us up for breakdowns when the majority of the ones used are "lower level." Mechanisms that worked in early development will wreck havoc in an adult's life, causing overreactions to some signals and a lack of attention to important ones. Poorly adapted defenses are no one's fault. But they are strong indicators of where symptoms could be originating

Examples of (problematic) Lower Level Defenses:

Projection:
"*My teddy bear got scared*" is announced by the child denying her own feeling, and projecting it outwards. *She's* not scared – but the bear is. As adults, we may project feelings onto another person, accusing someone else of doing what we secretly wish we could do. In a heated discussion, I begin to feel angry but withdraw fearfully, imagining it was the other person who suddenly got mad, not me.

Splitting, another troublesome defense, creates a world of extremes. The person consistently uses *black & white* thinking with no detectable shades of gray. Adore someone one day and despise him the next. Over-value people and then knock them off their pedestals with the same conviction. Again, remnants from early development – when a parent disappoints, "*I HATE YOU*" feels like a reasonable response for a four-year old. But hating and loving the same person is much too complicated, and will be perceived as dangerous. So we continue to see people as all good (what we want them to be all the time) or all bad (not up to my expectations and more importantly, not in my control). Black & white thinking makes things run smoothly – until something pops up that no longer fits either category.

Reality exists in zones of gray – which makes splitting a lousy long-term defense. It is also an especially hard one to change, because the unconscious mind looks for the simplest solution – such as creating a world comprised of only two categories. It certainly feels better than the dreaded option of no categories at all. To make decisions on a case-by-case basis, we need to trust more than our immediate judgment. We also need faith in our ability to *continue* making sound choices far into an unforeseeable future - too many unknowns in that picture to motivate change.

Control was probably a lifelong struggle for those of us who eventually break down – always needing to know what was coming (and *when* it was coming and how we were likely to feel the entire time it was here). Realizing the impossibility of that goal, we settled for the next best thing – fooling ourselves into *believing* we knew. And to accomplish that trick, we avoided all ambivalence. *We always know. We know exactly how we feel. We do not have negative feelings towards anyone we love, and we do not feel desire for anyone we hate. We are nothing if not clear on who we are and where we stand.*

The constraints tighten with the next set of dangerous thoughts:

3. **Thoughts too contradictory to self-image.**

Everyone lives with a self-image that is precious, while every minute encountering powerful desires that oppose it.

Human thoughts and emotions never sleep. As you read these words, you are constantly making links in stream of consciousness – within seconds, an image leads to a memory to a desire to a thought to a fear to a hope to an ideal to a sexual impulse to a wish to any angry thought to another memory.

The spontaneity of that process is stopped in its tracks by primitive defenses.

Condensation and **Displacement** (those features of primary process thinking) also act as defenses. **Displacement** is often at work in phobias – a powerful fear has been redirected into an unlikely external object or action – and as long as we avoid the phobic object (flying, snakes, heights, etc.) we will feel safe from the unnamed fear it represents. Not only do phobias offer us a sense of control over anxiety (it is within our power to simply refuse to fly, or to go anywhere near snake territory), they also let us avoid the thought that is being symbolized by the fear of flying or snakes. We find relief from it in effigy – by obsessing over the phobia that disguises it.

Condensation operates defensively in many symptoms – the key is to remember that many disturbing ideas can be packed into one symbol. A panic attack may be the compilation of anxieties – some from current life situations and some from long ago memories. There may be no conscious linking – sufferers are often unaware that a present day relationship or event has triggered past fears. The result is a *double whammy* of sensed danger that can explode in a single panic experience. (*"But why now? Nothing in my life is bad right now!"* But something in your present day life might be strongly reminiscent of an old unresolved danger).

Compartmentalization is used by nearly everyone to some degree. With this defense, we do not literally deny the existence of a dangerous thought, but shuffle our thoughts around so that no two contradictory ones can possibly collide. It is like putting certain thoughts and feelings into hermetically sealed containers while we busy ourselves with their nemesis. Then on command, we can reverse the situation. North and South never meet.

"No one on earth should ever *starve"* can exist alongside *"I **must** have this new speedboat"* long enough to write a check to the marina (without taking a single step to end world hunger). We are not at any point denying the reality of the other belief; we are just not thinking about it, and won't be until the coast is clear.

The ideals and values that make up a self-image fit poorly with many of our underlying motives. We want to believe we are good people and try to make choices that support that belief. Underneath, every one of us is still as selfish as we were at 5, and we want what we want when we *want* it. We feel envy and jealousy and rage at the very people we cherish. We want everyone to live in peace, but we also want to chase our own dreams and goals and aren't ready to sacrifice to the extent we feel we *should*. That is simply being human. The trouble arrives when we need to be better than human.

The more we cling to Absolutes (*This is how the world should always work; This is how everyone should act; This is who I am in every situation;)*, the more we will need to compartmentalize (otherwise the discrepant thoughts that could activate one another will keep producing anxiety until they are sealed off).

Overly-controlled thinking starts out as an anchoring platform making us feel stronger and more secure in who we are – but easily becomes a rope bridge to be crossed daily – in gale force winds. We will live in fear of any unexpected thought with the potential to shake the already fragile platform beneath our feet.

We know it is just a matter of time before *something* in ourselves will contradict our absolutes (or worse, confront us with real hypocrisy). A sense of humor is crucial. Imperfections - not only as in "failing short of a mark," but downright selfish hidden agendas – are human. The only option we have (without living inside a time bomb) is to find ways to make peace with our own duality.

Sometimes we're hypocrites.
Sometimes we desire someone we hate,
and despise someone we love.
We have fantasies about abusing the power we hold.
Sometimes we envy our children,
and have murderous thoughts towards our caretakers.
We may even cherish feeling like a victim when it gives us "good reasons" to be enraged (while still denying our own aggression).

The list would be endless.
Every human mind is filled with ambivalent thoughts.

Learning Your Triggers

When certain factors converge, symptoms intensify. There are **generic triggers** that apply to most of us:
- Lack of sleep;
- Excessive sleep;
- Poor eating habits;
- Disturbing movies, music, images;
- Isolation;
- Chronic self-monitoring.

One of those may be bearable – but add a second or a third, and bad results are guaranteed.

Other triggers seem to be **symptom-specific**:
- Hard-pounding exercise can make anxiety sufferers feel *worse*. Additional adrenaline is the last thing they need, and the physical sensations of racing heart, shortness of breath, changes in blood pressure, etc. can put too much attention on the body's status. *What does this burning in my side mean? Is something wrong with my heart?* And hypochrondriacal fears return with a vengeance. Moderate exercise for those sufferers – yoga, stretching, swimming makes much better sense.

- On the other hand, being too sedentary is bad for depressive symptoms. It increases the feelings of detachment/deadness of self. Heavy exercise can temporarily do wonders for negative moods because the release of adrenaline and endorphins by the hormonal system are mood *elevators*.

Finally, there will be **triggers unique to you**. Learn as much as you can about what seems to set you off – what thoughts or actions bring on each of the individual symptoms that cause you the greatest distress. The point here is not to *avoid* any and everything that might ever make you symptomatic, but to know what will aggravate a feeling state. It is a way of gaining control over what feels like utter lack of control, and in time may help you to realize that much of what happens during your worst times is coming from within you, predictable by you – not something falling on you out of nowhere.

Also explore psychological triggers:
There are certain situations that aggravate stress levels unique to each of us. Feeling trapped in a situation, or out of control, or furious, or jealousy, envious, competitive, etc. Pay attention to what seems to

increase strong emotions. Don't try to judge your triggers, or deny them with *"but everybody gets mad or jealous – I shouldn't get that upset."* It will take time to work on the reasons for your reactions, but in the meantime, be honest about how you seem to work. If something triggers a symptom, you need to know. You may not always be able to prevent an increase in anxiety or a sudden sense of overwhelm. You may spot trouble coming and be unable to stop it, but that will not always be the case. Learning how and why you seem to respond to given triggers is like constructing a map of your mind's patterns. Having a map is a step away from feeling helpless – and anything that puts you in control rather than being a passive responder is an important step towards recovery.

When therapy fails to make a dent:

Therapy Tip

By the way, do not expect *talking* to cure you. Sometimes we enter therapy and tell our stories - well-rehearsed and memorized a thousand times over. We keep internally repeating the same thinking that got us into this mess in the first place. Telling the same tales with the same morals that we have long held to be true will not incite change.

Change occurs when we find words for thoughts that have been unexpressed – not from repeating words that solidify old convictions.

We obsessive-types are so determined to keep seeing ourselves a certain way that we present the following challenge – we want to be fixed, but not altered. Cured, but not touched.

Some of us may be *petrified* of change, especially if it means being surprised by what we might see in ourselves.

When therapy works, we find a way to listen to our own words without needing to see what lies ahead.

More Suggestions:

1) **Learning to tolerate ambivalence:**
Every human being must find *some* way to live with:
- the unknown;
- pending death;
- risk/uncertainty;
- anxiety as part of the human condition.

How we handle *knowing and not knowing* the most frightening aspects of life will depend on what defenses we learn during development. Healthier people deal better with their fears, not that they have fewer of them.

The **inability to tolerate anxiety** is a problem born from efforts to ward off ambiguity. Over time, the trait becomes more damaging that the original anxiety would have been. Rather than moving *forward* while anxious, we stop everything and put all energy into removing the slightest feeling of uncertainty. That may require shifting reality around inside our minds, denying some obvious truths, distracting ourselves in self-destructive ways, or ruminating over disturbing thoughts with ferocity (in efforts to master them).

While it can be a good idea to reduce stress during recovery, no one can live in some anxiety-free box forever. The goal is to improve the methods used to *handle* it.

Keep an eye out for **ambivalent feelings** – remind yourself that it is not possible to exist without having conflicting thoughts about the people, things, and principles you value. Ironically, anxiety patients are especially frightened of that fact, because they believe confusion/inner conflict indicates mental illness, not sanity. We can make things even worse by trying to force ourselves into more rigid thought patterns while recovering – it is exactly the opposite of what will heal. Make efforts to face that there is much you do not know, even things about yourself. The goal is not to anticipate all the solutions and answers to future quandaries, but to trust yourself to navigate the unknown intact – being able to *not* know without assuming danger.

2) **Learning your Triggers** -
Notice what instigates your particular symptoms (or in extreme cases, a relapse of the breakdown). The things that are triggers for us will probably not change – our response to them can lessen, but whatever once set us off will remain a hot button. Watch for them, identify them and work with who you are.

3) **Watch for Smoke and Mirrors** -
You may begin to believe that the most important aspects of you are the horrible feelings that arrived in the breakdown. It can seem that symptoms now define you. That is nothing but a trick of the mind. Regardless of how you feel, a fully functional person is still within you -- intact, hiding perhaps, but unscathed. Once recovery picks up pace, a sense of genuine self returns. Until then, resist the urge to *identify* with your fears, obsessions and moods.

We get stronger by working *through* symptoms, not by embodying them.

Prolonged symptoms can act as subterfuge, continually pulling our focus to convince us that truth lies in constantly watching them – at the cost of avoiding other parts of ourselves.

In elaborate magic tricks, obvious movements are smoke screens for the *real* trick being manipulated out of sight. *Look! A shiny colorful scarf that swirls – keep your eye on it, watch how fast it flies*! while the magician's *other* hand fumbles for a lever to set up the next illusion.

Part of the mind relies on lingering symptoms to serve as distractions while it reconstructs faulty defenses behind the scenes. The more you gaze directly *into* those bizarre thoughts and sensations, the more you are being fooled. In the throes of highly dramatic symptoms, full distraction takes place. Whenever possible, keep your focus on the *other* hand.

Suggestions II Chart

What helps:	Remember:
Tolerating Anxiety/ Tolerating Ambivalence	Actively look for examples of ambiguity. Search out the moments you have strong opposing feelings towards valued people and ideas. The more you can integrate conflicting wishes into full awareness, the easier it becomes to stop thinking in black and white. And that, by strengthening your ability to tolerate normal anxiety, can speed up recovery by leaps & bounds.
Learning your triggers	If you keep a journal record the actions, thoughts or events that seem to increase your symptoms. Knowing what will likely activate them not only allows you to redirect, but offers tangible control (as opposed to the magical or illusionary control you may be relying on).
Keep an eye on the <u>other</u> hand	When you feel all your attention being pulled towards a overwhelming symptom, ask yourself: what would I have been doing right that minute if the symptom had not stopped me? It may be a clue to the hidden service that the symptom is providing. Also, notice what thoughts, feelings and activities have come to a halt since your breakdown. Watch for how your symptoms have changed you, and question what that change might have kept from happening.

Human beings are odd. We are silly, quirky, and sometimes bizarre. Remember that. As you recover from a breakdown, you may develop ridiculous expectations of yourself. Now that you have dipped into the "other side," you will not feel safe for awhile. Be on the lookout for efforts to appear *saner than sane*.

Is this a sign of another breakdown?

I can't believe I said that at work – am I losing control of my own actions?

I completely forgot I put this here... is something else happening to my mind?

This decision is impossible for me – normal people make decisions all the time – will I ever be normal??

I thought I was in love; but now, only a month later, I feel nothing for him! Is that a sign that I don't even know my own feelings?

You will *always* do oddball things – not because you had emotional trouble, but because you're human. Try to remember some of your less-than-stellar moments from long ago – way before the breakdown. Don't interpret idiosyncrasies as the development of some horrible new symptom. No one's actions and thoughts are models of normalcy.

I chatter away to my dog (and if he leaves the room, I stop – as if it would be odd to keep talking when he's not in earshot).

I leave clothes to soak in the sink and completely forget I did it - till about six hours later.

I make plans with someone, then change my mind, only to later remake them – and I'm *still* not sure if its something I really want to do.

I walk into the kitchen and have not one earthly clue what I was going in there to do. I still have a bizarre and highly vivid imagination. Sometimes I have nightmares. I'm capable of *very* dark fantasies. (and these are just the quirks I'm willing to admit in print).

Give yourself a break. Keep perspective. And when at all possible, keep a **sense of humor**.

Feeling Better, but...

Recovering from emotional pain is very different than healing from a physical ailment. Don't expect it to take place in an upward line on a graph.

There will be days where you feel normal again. There will be setbacks when you least expect them.

There will be times you feel stronger and happier than you ever did – even before the breakdown.

There will be hours where you're convinced you've never healed at all.

You will have faith and hope in yourself.
You will sabotage your own progress.
You will realize you're finally taking control of your own life.
You will feel as helpless as a child.

It's part of getting well – and the ups and downs are not futile – you're learning to improve your own resiliency.

You're learning that regardless of how terrified you've been, you are nowhere near as fragile as you feared.

You're learning that you can survive your own feelings – without any damage being done.

You're learning to trust *yourself* to carry you through this life.

It feels erratic and some days it will feel utterly hopeless.
You're learning – which is part of the process. We each heal on our own schedule.

Printed in the United Kingdom
by Lightning Source UK Ltd.
118724UK00001B/98